EXTRAORDINARY WOMEN EXPLORERS

THE WOMEN'S HALL OF FAME SERIES

EXTRAORDINARY WOMEN EXPLORERS

by Frances Rooney

Second Story Press

Library and Archives Canada Cataloguing in Publication

Rooney, Frances
Extraordinary women explorers / by Frances Rooney.

(The women's hall of fame series)
Includes bibliographical references.

ISBN 1-896764-98-3

1. Women explorers--Biography--Juvenile literature.
I. Title. II. Series: Women's hall of fame series.

G200.R65 2005 j910'.92'2 C2005-900547-5

Edited by Carroll Klein
Designed by Laura McCurdy

Cover photographs credited on page 117

Printed and bound in Canada

Second Story Press gratefully acknowledges the support of the Ontario Arts Council and the Canada Council for the Arts for our publishing program. We acknowledge the financial support of the Government of Canada through the Book Publishing Industry Development Program, and the Government of Ontario through the Ontario Media Development Corporation's Ontario Book Initiative.

40 YEARS + 40 ANS
ONTARIO ARTS COUNCIL
CONSEIL DES ARTS DE L'ONTARIO

Canada Council for the Arts
Conseil des Arts du Canada

Published by
SECOND STORY PRESS
20 Maud Street, Suite 401
Toronto, Ontario, Canada
M5V 2M5

www.secondstorypress.ca

The author can be contacted at frooney2002@yahoo.com

TABLE OF CONTENTS

to
Lois F. Watson
again

Introduction

What draws people to explore? Most of us, faced with danger, poor food, extreme heat or cold, lack of money, and the possibility of illness or even death, would probably run home to a warm bed and three meals a day. And yet, for the thrill of the journey, many adventurous individuals face their fears and welcome, even seek out, the mysteries of the unknown—from bandits and wolves to frostbite and starvation.

Exploration and adventure, often considered the realm of men, have always attracted women. In this book, you will meet women who refused to let the added difficulties of being a *woman* explorer keep them from following their dreams. The unknown called to them and they answered.

Why do women keep returning to the unknown, some of them over a period of sixty or seventy years? First, there is curiosity. Freya Stark became more and more curious as she went along, saying, "Curiosity ought to increase as one gets older." Then there is the lure of faraway places. Freya said of that, "The beckoning counts, and not the clicking of the latch behind you: and all through life that actual moment of emancipation still holds that delight, of the whole world coming to meet you like a wave." And the challenge. Alexandra David-Néel put it this way: "I was inspired by the desire to do something no one else had and to try myself physically and intellectually." There is also the fascination of the journey itself: "The snow peaks, the silence, the contentment, the clear air, the sense of exhilaration and energy and peace," as Dervla Murphy put it. And sometimes these women took into account the importance of being women explorers. Alexandra David-Néel wrote, "All sights, all things which are Lhasa's own beauty and peculiarity, would have to be seen by the lone woman explorer who had the nerve to come to them from afar, the first of her sex."

Many of the famous male explorers went through the world claiming territories, conquering peoples, and destroying cultures. Part of what sets people apart as explorers, and in particular as *women* explorers, is their attitude toward what they are doing and toward the places they go and the people they meet.

Almost all women explorers have pointedly and repeatedly expressed their awe, respect, and appreciation for the places that they have gone and the people they have met. These women did not want to claim or conquer anyone or anything. In our world, where there is so much violence both against people and against our delicate environment, this attitude is a huge gift. Matty McNair put it very clearly after she and Denise Martin led the Women's Relay to the North Pole: "We didn't conquer the Arctic; we came to move across it and to learn from it." Edith Watson photographed people who were at ease with her in a way that can only happen when people think highly of each other. Victoria Hayward's writings speak vividly of and with great respect for the many cultures among New Canadians. She judges no one, feels no sense of superiority, is interested only to observe and learn, not to change people but to be changed by them. Amanda Berry Smith was happy to talk with people whether they accepted what she said or not. Sharon

Wood made the connection between the inner and outer journey: "Climbers don't conquer mountains. The conquest occurs within the mind of the climber, in penetrating those self-imposed barriers of fears, doubts and limitations, and getting through to that good stuff—that stuff called potential, most of which we rarely use." Freya Stark noted that she went not to prove or teach anything but to observe and learn. Phyllis Munday went to both climb mountains and learn things that she could share with others. Alexandra David-Néel went on a personal and spiritual journey as well as a physical one, and shared her discoveries in a way that taught the Western world about the East and about Buddhism. The challenge and the reward for these women is in the expansion of the human spirit, not political conquest. As Freya Stark wrote, "This is a great moment, when you see, however distant, the goal of your wandering ... It matters not how many ranges, rivers, or parching, dusty ways may lie between you: it is yours now forever."

Two of the women in this book lived into their hundredth year. Others also lived long and well. Still others continue to travel, explore, and seek new people and places; age does not seem to tie them down. In addition to being explorers they were geographers, cartographers, historians, anthropologists, botanists, photographers, mothers, and well-known writers. It seems that pursuing physical and intellectual challenge and following your dreams contributes to a long and full life.

The women in this book, who explored over a period of almost two hundred years, have many sisters in spirit and action. Sharon Wood was the sixth woman to climb Mount Everest—the first we know of was Junko Tabei, from Japan, in 1975. Alexandra David-Néel's routes crossed and recrossed those of Isabella Bird Bishop thirty years earlier.

In 1985 a twenty-four-year-old Australian, Sorrell Wilby, set out to walk from Tibet to Lhasa, a distance of 2880 kilometers (1800 miles).

Nor were the places the women in this book went the only areas women have explored. Dervla Murphy crossed Africa at its widest point from east to west. More than two hundred years earlier, Isabel Gramson Godin set out to walk across South America from west to east. In the early 1930s, Violet Cressy started at the Atlantic side and went up the Amazon. In the 1880s, Florence Dixie explored Patagonia, at the southern tip of South America. In 1977 Jane Stanger went to Madagascar for a year. She is still there. In 2004 Canadian Jody James walked the Australian Outback. As I write this, Matty McNair is leading a sixty-day expedition to the South Pole. These are some of the women we know of. There are hundreds more ...

Sacagawea

1790(?)–1884

No one knows how old Sacagawea was when, in 1805 and 1806, she accompanied the Lewis and Clark Expedition across the American plains and through the mountains to the Pacific Ocean, but she was probably no more than fourteen or fifteen. This voyage and her contribution to the expedition earned her a place in both the history and the mythology of the American West.

Born in what is now central Montana in the United States, Sacagawea grew up learning the ways of her nation and living the nomadic life of her tribe, the Shoshone. In

The name "Sacagawea" means Bird Woman and was given to her by her captors. Nobody knows what her original Shoshone name might have been. Because "Sacagawea" is a phonetic spelling of a Minetaree word, it has sometimes been interpreted as "Sakakawea" or "Sacajawea" instead.

summer the Shoshone people lived on the berries, fish, and wild game of the eastern Rockies. In winter they moved down to the plains east of the mountains to hunt larger animals, including buffalo.

When Sacagawea was eleven or twelve, and while the men were away hunting, an enemy tribe, the Minetaree, raided the Shoshone camp, killing some of the women and children and taking others as slaves. Sacagawea and a friend had been picking berries by the river, and they tried to get away by hiding in the trees at the banks and fleeing downstream. Sacagawea was captured; her friend disappeared.

The Minetaree took Sacagawea east to their village, in what is now the state of North Dakota. There she lived in slavery until she was married to Toussaint Charbonneau, a French-Canadian fur trader who won her in a card game. Charbonneau treated Sacagawea badly and she continued to work like a slave. Soon, in 1804, Sacagawea became pregnant.

Far to the east in the new United States, Thomas Jefferson had been elected president in 1802. He had long dreamed of annexing part of the Louisiana Territory west of the Mississippi River, then owned by the French. In 1803, France agreed to sell the entire territory for $15 million. The purchase more than doubled the size of the new country.

Jefferson obtained $2,500 from Congress to sponsor an expedition to explore and map the new territory and to observe and record its plant and animal life. After a year of preparation, the forty-five men of the Lewis and Clark Expedition, with supplies and several large canoes, left

St. Louis, Missouri, and headed north and west, up the Missouri River, into the unknown.

A young Shoshone woman in the late 1800s.

Sacagawea's husband, Charbonneau, heard about the expedition and offered his services as a translator to Lewis and Clark. His original plan was to go alone, but when the organizers hesitated, he told them that he had two wives who belonged to the Shoshone Nation, across whose land the expedition would have to travel. His wives could help them pass peacefully through the area and could also help them buy the horses they would badly need by the time they got there. Lewis and Clark agreed to take Charbonneau on as long as one of his wives also came.

Sacagawea's baby, Jean-Baptiste, quickly nicknamed Pomp (which means first-born in Shoshone), was born on February 11, 1805. When he was just a few weeks old, the expedition left, and Pomp travelled in a pouch strapped to his mother's body.

Sacagawea's skills were soon needed. When food grew scarce, she found roots and edible plants in the forests. The expedition ate over a hundred pounds of meat a day, so her knowledge of the animals they could hunt was crucial. At times, it was Sacagawea and Lewis's Newfoundland dog, Scammon, who kept the men fed: Sacagawea by providing fresh fruits and berries that, although no one knew it at the time, kept the dreaded disease scurvy away, and the dog by tracking large animals and catching squirrels, beaver, and small game.

With spring and thawing ice and snow, the Missouri

River flowed faster, and the rapids became increasingly treacherous. The members of the expedition needed all their strength and skill to keep going. Once, while Sacagawea was travelling in the largest of the three boats (known as *pirogues*), a gust of wind came up and almost overturned it. Not long after, a storm hit, and the sail ripped away from the man who was tending it. Then the boat started to fill with water and Charbonneau, never a brave man, panicked at the helm. Only when an expedition member held him at gunpoint did he again grab the rudder and steer the boat while others bailed water. By that time, the captain's journals and all the expedition's papers, navigation instruments, medicine, and goods to trade and give to the First Nations people they encountered had fallen into the river. Sacagawea first made sure that Pomp was secure, then reached into the foaming water, even though the boat was still in danger of sinking, and retrieved everything she could. Lewis praised her courage and quick thinking and said that Sacagawea had saved things that were worth his life, perhaps all their lives.

As the group of forty-five men, their two leaders, and Sacagawea and Pomp went up the Missouri, Lewis and Clark named rivers after members of the group. They named one particularly pretty stream the Sacagawea River.

By June, the travellers were miserable from mosquitoes, gnats, fleas, lack of food, muddy water, and the threat of grizzly bears and rattlesnakes. Even the dog was miserable from insect bites and sharp thorns in his paws. Several of the men became ill. Sacagawea, too, developed a high fever and stomach cramps. For several days Clark bled her by opening one of her veins and keeping it open.

When Sacagawea's son Pomp was older, Lewis educated him in Europe, where he learned several languages before returning to North America to work as a guide in the northwest.

He gave her a strong laxative and opium. These were accepted medical practices of the day, but they just made her worse. Soon it was clear to everyone, including Sacagawea, that without some drastic change, she would die. After six days of high fever and bleeding, her pulse was faint, and her fingers and arms twitched. Lewis, who had been away, returned, saw how sick Sacagawea was, and gave her healing bark and mineral water. She got better enough to refuse all further treatment, and after a few more days she was sitting up, eating soup and buffalo meat. During the several weeks it took to carry the boats and supplies around the Great Falls of the Missouri and continue upriver, Sacagawea stayed in camp and regained her strength.

In the 1800s it was common practice to cut sick people so that the disease would leave their body with the 'bad' blood.

Soon after the group started out again, they came to an area of deep canyons with almost vertical sides. The only way past them was to go down into each canyon and then up the other side. Sacagawea climbed them with Pomp strapped to her.

On June 29, 1805, as they started to climb out of one of these canyons, a gentle rain turned into a furious thunderstorm with huge hailstones. They took refuge under a large boulder, but rocks began hurtling down the sides of the canyon and deeper and deeper streams of water rushed around their feet and legs. If they were going to survive, they had to get to the top of the canyon. The rain ripped Pomp from his carrier, and Sacagawea carried him with one arm, hanging onto the cliff with the other. Charbonneau saved himself. Clark pushed Sacagawea ahead of him, and he, Sacagawea, and Pomp made it to the top.

When the party reached Shoshone territory, Lewis took three men and headed off to look for Sacagawea's people

> "The Indian woman who has been of great service to me as a pilot through this country recommends a gap in the mountains more south, which I shall cross," wrote Clark in his diary.

and the horses the expedition now needed if they were ever to get to the Pacific. They were gone for almost a month. The Shoshones they saw ran away at the approach of these strangers. The men needed Sacagawea to make the contact.

She found the Shoshone camp and, taking Pomp, Lewis, Clark, and a few others with her, approached. Seeing her, her people did not run away. Then a young woman rushed up to Sacagawea: she was the friend who had been with Sacagawea when the Minetaree had captured her. Her friend had been named Jumping Fish for the way she had fled the marauders through the water.

Later in the day, Lewis and Clark needed Sacagawea to interpret for them when they met with the chief. She translated Shoshone into Minetaree, her husband translated the Minetaree to French, and one of the soldiers translated the French into English. As the meeting began and the chief spoke, Sacagawea recognized his voice: he was her brother. She and Cameahwait embraced, and she wrapped him in her blanket in a gesture of affection. She asked about other members of her family, and he told her that only one other brother and a nephew were still alive. Sacagawea, Bird Woman, had come home.

The expedition stayed with the Shoshone to visit and to buy horses. Even though they needed Sacagawea's knowledge of the terrain, Lewis and Clark were willing for her to stay there with her people. Much to their relief, she chose to accompany them the rest of the way. This meant crossing the Rocky Mountains and travelling to the Great Water, the Pacific Ocean, in the west.

It was September, and snow had already fallen in the mountains. There was little food, and the men ate any roots or berries Sacagawea could find. The going was treacherous and a mistake could mean that they would freeze in the mountains and might never be found. In places the trail had to be cut with axes.

When food gave out the expedition ate candles. Slowly they continued, most of the men sick or hurt. Clark had injured his hip and could barely walk, and Lewis was sick. Sacagawea found whatever bits she could for the men to eat, taking care of herself and Pomp all the way.

Finally the trail started to descend. They had survived the winter and the mountains. There were fish, streams of running water, and trees to make into boats. On the way up the Missouri River they had met few other people. Now there were scattered tribes of Shoshone with whom Sacagawea could make first contact. Since a woman was with the men, the tribes knew that they came in peace. Clark wrote in his journal, "This sight of this Indian woman ... [assured] these people of our friendly intentions ... no woman ever accompanied a war party in this quarter." The expedition went down the Columbia River until it grew wider and wider. Finally it was impossible to see the sides of the river and the water became salty. They had made it to the Pacific.

There are more statues of Sacagawea in the U.S. than of any other woman. This one is in North Dakota.

They set up camp close to the ocean, in what is now Astoria, Oregon. English, Spanish, Americans, and Russians had been there before them, but had always arrived by sea: no non-First Nations people had ever travelled from the east by land. The expedition spent the winter preparing for the return trip. One day a whale washed up on the shore near their camp. Sacagawea had heard about whales, huge fish that breathe air and are bigger than four or five buffalo. When Charbonneau said he would not take her to the ocean to see it, she spoke to Captain Clark and the two of them went. Sacagawea spoke of the ocean and of that whale for the rest of her life.

On March 23, 1806, the group started back. This trip, too, was difficult and relied on the wild food that Sacagawea found. They took a different route through Shoshone territory and did not see Sacagawea's people as they passed through. Charbonneau decided to go to St. Louis where Clark had promised to find him work. (Clark also offered to pay for Pomp's education when the time came, and he did.) Charbonneau received $533.33 1/3 for his work with the expedition. Sacagawea was paid nothing.

After living briefly in St. Louis, Charbonneau returned to the wilderness and Sacagawea began her travels. Charbonneau was last seen in 1839. Sometime between then and 1842 he died.

Some stories say that Sacagawea died young, at about twenty-five. It is now generally believed, however, that it was Charbonneau's other Shoshone wife who died, and that Sacagawea lived into her late eighties. Stories and other records tell that she lived for a time with various tribes in Canada, then with the Comanche in Oklahoma for about twenty-five years, leaving there in 1855. From there she spent six years with the Bannock tribe in southern Idaho, after which she went to stay with a Ute friend outside the present site of Laramie, Wyoming. In 1865, Shoshones passed through there and Sacagawea went with them to spend the last years of her life on the Wind River Reservation in western Wyoming. It seems that by the end of her life she was fluent in at least three languages

Sacagawea's grave, center, at the Wind River Cemetery near Fort Washakie, Wyoming. Pomp's grave and that of another son, Bazil, are on either side.

(Shoshone, Comanche, and French), that she said little about her early life, and that she was respected for her quiet wisdom.

There are more statues of Sacagawea in the United States than of any other woman. They are spread from St. Louis to the West Coast, and they tell of the courage of this translator and guide of the Lewis and Clark Expedition. Without Sacagawea's knowledge of the land and its peoples, the expedition would not have explored and recorded the Louisiana Territory, and would not have made it to the Pacific Ocean and back.

Amanda Berry Smith

1837–1915

AMANDA BERRY WAS BORN INTO SLAVERY IN MARYLAND, not far from Washington, D.C., on January 23, 1837. Her parents were slaves on adjoining estates, but by the time she was four, her father had managed to buy his freedom. Over the next few years he bought freedom for his wife, Amanda, and her younger brother and sister. Ten more children would be born as what were known as "Free Blacks." Amanda was the oldest of these thirteen children.

Life was not easy for Free Blacks. Earning a living was difficult, and people lived in fear of being kidnapped back into slavery. By 1850 the Berry family had moved to York County, Pennsylvania. Even though it was illegal for slaves to read and write, both Amanda's parents, Miriam and Samuel, were among the many who learned (it was often the lady of the plantation who taught and encouraged slaves to read and write). In turn, Amanda's parents taught her at home. As the oldest daughter she needed to help with the younger children and, as soon as possible, she needed to earn money. In all, Amanda attended school for only a few months.

The Berrys' house in Pennsylvania was one of the major stops for the Underground Railway. Some nights Amanda's father would meet fifteen to twenty men in his field and take them to the next stop as they fled slavery for freedom in Canada. Slave owners valued the people they (and the law) considered their "property," and often went to great lengths to recapture those who ran away. The owners sometimes even hired bounty hunters with bloodhounds to track escaped slaves. The Berry family risked their own safety to help people get away. One night men with dogs showed up at the Berrys' door. The dogs had tracked an escaped slave to the family's house, and the bounty hunters found him there and took him back. Another time, Miriam Berry hid a man between the mattress and the rope frame of the bed that Amanda's little brother was sleeping in. When the hunters demanded to know who was in the bed, Miriam threw back the covers. The hunters saw the sleeping baby and went away. Amanda was glad her family helped the runaway slaves. She also knew how dangerous it was for both the family and the people they helped.

Runaway slaves used many kinds of codes to tell each other the route to Canada. Most notably, these were in the songs we know as spirituals and in the design and pictures on quilts. A quilt could be a map to freedom.

At thirteen, Amanda got a job as a

domestic and at sixteen she married. The marriage was unhappy, and when the U.S. Civil War broke out in 1861, her husband left to join a Black brigade in the Northern Army. He may have died or he may have chosen not to go home; either way, he never returned.

After the war Amanda married James Henry Smith, a deacon in the African Methodist Episcopal Church (AME) in Philadelphia, and took his last name. He died not long after, but the widowed Amanda was only getting started with her adventures. For the next forty-three years she was active in the AME Church, preaching and teaching in countless places in North America, Europe, Asia, and Africa.

From 1869 to 1878 Amanda preached in AME churches along the east coast of the U.S. She then spent a year in England and two years in India, mostly in Calcutta. She spoke publicly and preached in churches and rented halls. At first, audiences may have gone to see her because she was a woman from America who had been born a slave. Once they heard her speak, though, they loved her. She drew huge crowds and became known throughout India.

In 1881, after a short time back in England, Amanda left for Africa, where she lived and explored for the next nine years, mostly in Liberia and Sierra Leone. She didn't make maps or discover unknown places. Her real gift as an explorer was her ability to go into remote villages and get to know the people and how they lived in a way that no other outsider had ever done. Did Amanda have an easier time meeting people because she was Black, as were the people she met? We don't really know. It may have helped, but there were many Black missionaries in Africa at the time. What seems to have set her apart was that she totally accepted the people she met for who they were,

The churches paid their Black missionaries less than white ones, women less than men.

and enjoyed being with them. She was happy to entertain them with stories, including religious stories, but she did not try to convert people to her way of thinking. She treasured spending time with people in their villages, she liked and valued the people she met, and they liked her. She saw things she would not have seen if the people she visited were cautious around her. She travelled fearlessly, staying with welcoming communities for several days or weeks before wandering to the next village. She shared her experiences with her colleagues and with readers in the U.S., Britain, and India by publishing articles and an autobiography.

Amanda's travels in Africa developed a pattern: she would speak at churches in a town or city and visit with the residents and local church and government officials, who were usually European and American. Many people spoke English but Amanda sometimes needed to use an

A sketch from Amanda's autobiography, showing Amanda herself sitting in the shade and teaching local children during her time in Liberia. The sketch was titled, "My first Sunday School, Plukie, Cape Palmas."

interpreter. Once she had visited for a while in a Westernized area, she would go off into remote territory and visit people who didn't care about urban centers or colonial governments. She would live with rural Africans and speak to them about their lives and her religion. In the countryside, most people had heard about Christianity and the missionaries. The people who lived in the places she visited welcomed Amanda, listened to her out of curiosity and politeness, enjoyed her company, then went back to life as it had always been. She decided early in her travels that her biggest value for the people she encountered was as a few hours' entertainment. Everyone had a good time, and for Amanda that was enough.

Long distances were generally travelled by ship, which was not Amanda's favorite method of transportation: she always got desperately seasick. Aside from that, Africa, its people and landscape, enchanted her. "This is Africa, and I am here!" she wrote, hardly believing her good fortune. Another time she wrote, "It was a lovely moonlit night such as I have seen only in Africa; for I think the moon is more lovely here than anywhere I ever saw it. I thought it was beautiful in India. But, oh! the moonlight in Africa. It was still and light."

Amanda liked the food, but it took over a year for her digestive system to get used to it. She fell ill with fevers on several occasions. Once, after eight years in Africa, she became ill and was unable to eat. She found herself dreaming about the food of home: "I wanted a nice broiled mutton chop, basted with some nice hard butter, not that soft, oily stuff that was in the tins. I wanted a nice baker's roll, with hard butter off the ice, and a nice cup of tea, with some fresh cream, not condensed milk." Then one day she woke up, happily ate the food that was available, and was fine. Nothing would stop her constant journeying.

Amanda adopted two children during her travels in Africa. The first was a girl, Frances, whose mother had died. In Liberia she later adopted a second child, Bob. At the time of their adoptions, Bob was about six years old, and Frances a little older. They travelled with her and later went to school in England and the U.S.

In one village Amanda witnessed a trial for witchcraft. The chief's main wife, the queen, had been accused of bewitching a fourteen-year-old girl. The girl was bitten by a snake and died, and according to the girl's mother, this was the queen's fault. The queen was tried and found guilty, and a date was set for her execution. There was nothing Amanda could do to help, but her heart went out to the woman, whose calm dignity Amanda found impressive. Death was to be by drinking poison made from the local *sassy* wood. The queen had to drink two gallons of the mixture. If by some chance she survived that, she would have to drink another two gallons. If she drank three times in all, a total of six gallons, and survived, she would be considered innocent and allowed to live.

The queen picked up the jug and slowly drank. The mixture went down. And came back up again. She drank a second time, and the same thing happened. Then a third. Once again, the mixture came back up. No one knew why she survived, but she did, and was reinstated in the community. With great relief, Amanda went on her way.

She saw villages with rows of skulls lined up to protect the residents. She saw girls bought and sold as property, a reminder of the slavery her father had saved her from. She saw all kinds of rituals that were central to the lives of the people she visited. Often she and her various travelling companions walked from village to village. Sometimes they rode in

Amanda Berry Smith had five children, four of whom died. Later she adopted two more children in Africa.

carts, and once they had a carriage pulled by a bull who danced back and forth, into and out of the river with Amanda and her friend hanging on tightly. Eventually the bull settled down and they reached their destination.

And so Amanda wandered—exploring, teaching, meeting people, and visiting villages. If there were religious men in the area, sometimes they would not let her preach, saying that women should be silent in church. When that happened she taught children. She knew that she had a gift for speaking and found it foolish that men with less ability than she had wanted to keep her from using her God-given gift.

Amanda's departure from Africa in 1890 was delayed by the need to stay away from Cape Palmas for several weeks. A smallpox epidemic was raging through the area, and it was not safe to travel. Several of the Americans and British she knew, and huge numbers of native-born people, died. When the epidemic finally passed, she was glad to get on the ship for England.

Back in the U.S., Amanda lived in Harvey, Illinois, just outside Chicago. When she saw the same kind of poverty and neglect in Chicago that she had seen in Africa, she felt she had to do something about it. In 1895 she opened an orphanage. But she knew that a place to live was not enough. The children needed to learn skills and trades in order to avoid lives of poverty, so she also started an industrial school. She ran both the orphanage and the school until she died in 1915, at the age of seventy-eight.

Amanda was active with Frances Willard in the Women's Christian Temperance Union (WCTU), which fought for the prohibition of alcoholic drinks in the U.S. Because drunkenness was a major contributor to the abuse of women and children, the WCTU was also one of the earliest organizations in the U.S. to fight for women's rights.

Amanda Berry Smith helped slaves escape their bondage, travelled the earth, spoke to audiences in North America, Europe, Asia, and Africa, went places and met people in Africa in a way no other outsider had ever done, wrote a hugely popular five-hundred-page autobiography, and provided a home and schooling for African-American children. She may have been born in slavery, but she lived her life as only a woman who is free in her heart and mind can live.

Edith S. Watson and Victoria Hayward

1861–1943 1876–1958

As soon as Edith Watson finished high school, she took the family donkey, Jaffa, and the donkey cart and left home for two weeks on the road. It was her first trip, and it cost a total of five dollars. Although she didn't know it at the time, it was the beginning of more than sixty years of travel and exploration.

Edith Sarah Watson was born on November 5, 1861, the youngest of Sarah and Reed Watson's four children. Sarah's family were part owners of the Hartford, Connecticut

Edith as a young girl.

newspaper, and Reed farmed tobacco in Connecticut and worked as a printer in Boston, Massachusetts. When Reed was away working, Sarah ran the farm. At sixteen, Edith's oldest sister Rosa went to work as a botanical artist at Harvard University. Her brother Don died at twenty, and Amelia, who was five years older than Edith, went to teach in northern New York state, so by the time she was thirteen or fourteen, Edith was the only child at home.

They were a happy family, even though money tended to be scarce. Reed believed that women should be shrewd with money, Sarah wanted her daughters to do whatever they wished with their lives, and both parents encouraged their children to be independent. Edith and Amelia, knowing that they would have to support themselves financially, created jobs for themselves doing what they loved.

All the Watson children received good educations. Don spoke to the farm animals in Latin. Rosa became a well-known painter of precise botanical drawings in her late teens. Amelia taught painting in a boarding school and later at summer institutes, which provided post-secondary education for women in the late nineteenth century. Edith went to one of the first high schools for women in the U.S., the Hartford Female Seminary. Her studies there included literature, history, art, mathematics, chemistry, physics, Latin, and French.

Edith, with Jaffa the donkey, explored Connecticut and Massachusetts in the summer of 1881. When she got home, she took up what she thought would be her career. She and her sister Amelia built a studio onto the family house, Amelia left her teaching job, and the sisters set up as working artists. For the next ten years, they painted and travelled around New England, showing and selling their paintings. They loved travelling and meeting people, established good reputations, and their paintings sold well.

One of Edith Watson's teachers at Hartford Female Seminary was Harriet Beecher Stowe, the author of *Uncle Tom's Cabin.*

But this all changed in the early 1890s, as the sisters went their separate ways. While Edith and Amelia continued to use the house in Connecticut as a home base, Amelia taught painting on Cape Cod in the summers and travelled to the southern U.S. to paint and show her work in galleries in the winters, usually in North Carolina or Florida.

Edith went north, and traded in her paintbrushes for a camera. In the early 1890s she started going to Newfoundland and Labrador between Easter and American Thanksgiving in November. In her travels she took pictures of rural people, often women or children, usually while they were working. Her photographs from these years show women making soap and bread, drying fish, harvesting crops, and carrying water home from the town well. We see men making barrels, repairing fish nets, maintaining ships, cutting up and processing a whale. Everywhere the children are working, too: helping with soap making, carrying water, pushing carts of food. The photographs she took show a world that has disappeared, and they provide us with a documented history of how people lived in those days.

Edith travelled by train, cart, horse, and donkey, or on foot, ferries, fishing boats, and rowboats. She made friends and boarded with local people, once even staying in a house built on stilts on the rocks out over the ocean. And she returned to Newfoundland, year after year, for almost twenty years.

Edith had found the way she would make her living. She sold photographs to magazines and newspapers in Canada, the U.S., and Britain. She exchanged photographs for food, lodging, and transportation—for trains, small boats, ships, and for the other kinds of transportation people of the area provided. She sold her photographs of ships' riggings to the rope companies whose rope was used in the rigging. She provided the photography for travel brochures for the governments of Newfoundland and Nova Scotia. She sent photographs to Kodak in Rochester, New York, in exchange for film, printing paper, and cameras. When she took pictures of barrels, the barrel companies found room and board for her when she was in town. The prices she could charge were not high, between fifty cents and two dollars for each photograph. But she worked constantly, sold thousands of prints, and managed to both pay for her wanderings and send money home.

Soon after 1900, Edith expanded her explorations to Nova Scotia and New Brunswick on Canada's east coast, including Grand Manan and Anticosti islands and the French-owned island colony of St. Pierre and Miquelon. From there she went on to Quebec, where she stayed with First Nations people in their villages and towns and visited the more populated areas. Percé Rock on the Gaspé Peninsula was a favorite place. She wandered all along the St. Lawrence River and, as she had done in Newfoundland, stayed with families on farms and in villages.

Edith S. Watson always insisted that her name, including her middle initial, appear with her published photographs. Because of this, it is possible to find her work in the magazines and newspapers she published in. Without that, we would not know who took those thousands of photographs.

Each year during this period of her life, Edith stayed in Connecticut between Thanksgiving and Christmas, and then went to Bermuda until just before Easter. Bermuda, a British colony and playground of the rich, was very different from rural Canada. Edith's purpose there, however, was not to play. She had a studio where she hand-painted photographs she had taken in Canada and sold her work. When the manager of the Bermudiana Hotel, the largest and most luxurious hotel on the island, invited her to sell her photographs in the lobby of the hotel, she did so for several years.

It was in Bermuda in 1911 that Edith met Victoria Hayward. Victoria, a math teacher at a boys' private school in New York, had returned home to Bermuda and become a journalist. She visited Edith in Connecticut the next summer, and the two lived and worked together for the rest of their lives. Edith took photographs and Victoria wrote articles. Although Edith continued to sell her photographs independently, she and Victoria also published many illustrated articles in magazines and newspapers. In 1921, they published their book, *Romantic Canada.* In the book Victoria Hayward coined the phrase, "the Canadian mosaic," which has been used ever since to describe Canada's multicultural nature.

A photograph that Edith took around 1900, of a girl carrying water in Hermitage, a Newfoundland outport. The hoop around the girl's skirts kept the buckets from tipping or banging against her legs.

Victoria fishing at Percé Rock on a trip to the Gaspé Peninsula.

Edith and Victoria travelled together to Newfoundland and Labrador and retraced Edith's journeys to Quebec. Then they branched out and went west. And north. They camped in the bush in northern Ontario. At the French River they stayed at a Canadian Pacific Railway construction camp. Once again, First Nations people fed and housed them.

They went to Manitoba and saw New Canadians (another phrase of Victoria's) growing beets and onions, making their way in their adopted land. The pair visited with Mennonites who had fled oppression in Russia and whose refusal to fight in wars (they believed in pacifism) would later create problems for them in Canada.

When World War I broke out in Europe in 1914, travel became more difficult, but this did not stop Edith and Victoria. Instead of going further west, they went to Parrsboro, outside Halifax, Nova Scotia. From there they sailed the east coast of Canada and photographed people fishing and drying fish, repairing nets, and making barrels. At Halifax Harbour, Edith hired boys who rowed small boats from which she took pictures of the ships. Almost all sailing ships had been taken off the water and replaced by more modern ones. During the war, however, every available vessel was needed, so many of these old ships were brought out and repaired and used to carry lumber to England. This was Edith's chance to see these disappearing vessels and capture them on film.

After the war it became almost impossible to exchange photographs for equipment, travel, and places to stay. Prices did not go up for photographs, so Edith, now almost sixty, had to work harder than ever. She and Victoria went back to northern Manitoba, sometimes following the railroad tracks from one isolated settlement to the next, often camping alone in the wilderness.

And they kept going west. Edith took pictures of people harvesting wheat in Saskatchewan and climbing mountains in Alberta. For two years she wrote letters to Peter Verigin, the leader of the Doukhobor people who, like the Mennonites in Manitoba, had fled religious persecution in Russia. The Canadian government did not treat the Doukhobors well, and like the Mennonites, many of them didn't stay in Canada but moved on to Central and South America. Those Doukhobors who did stay in Canada lived in groups of families, usually about seventy-five people, in communes in isolated areas of Alberta and British Columbia. The government had promised them good land, but they were given the poorest and rockiest land in those areas. Still, they created prosperous farms. The Doukhobors greeted few visitors from the outside, but they invited Edith and Victoria to spend the summers of 1919, 1920, and 1921 living with them in their communes. Edith was allowed to photograph the people and their lives. Her hundreds of pictures recorded and reveal a way of life that has now been lost.

Edith and Victoria didn't stop there. They went through the mountains and to the coast of British Columbia. They explored Vancouver Island, and some of Edith's photographs resemble the paintings Emily Carr did in that same area.

Margaret Morley, a close friend of Edith, Amelia, and Victoria, was a botanist, a writer of books on plants and insects, and the agricultural consultant to the British government in the West Indies.

From there they went to Haida Gwaii, which the English explorers called the Queen Charlotte Islands, and stayed with the Haida people. From parts of Haida Gwaii, it is possible on a clear day to see across the water to Alaska. Edith and Victoria went there, too. Always, Edith's photographs showed her respect for people and for the dignity of their work. Without her photographs, and the magazines, newspapers, companies, and governments that published them, many groups of Canadians would have gone totally un-noticed in the larger world.

The Great Depression hit in 1929, and the market for Edith's work almost disappeared. In 1931 she turned seventy. While she continued to sell all the photographs she could, it was time to stop wandering in the wild. Her mother had bought a cottage on Cape Cod in the 1880s. Edith, Victoria, and Amelia spent much time there together. Then in January 1933, Amelia went to Florida to set up a show of her paintings in a gallery. Walking to the gallery early one afternoon, she had a heart attack and died on the street.

Edith, left, and Victoria. This is one of the few photographs in existence showing Edith with a camera.

Edith and Victoria now travelled around New England and the east coast of the U.S. In 1943, on the way to Florida, Edith became ill and died shortly afterward. Victoria took the train back to Connecticut with the casket. They arrived on Christmas morning, 1943.

Victoria Hayward stayed in the house in Connecticut long enough to deal with Edith's will and the headstone for her grave. Then one day she left the house as if she were going for a walk. She never went back. Victoria moved to the cottage on Cape Cod and lived there until she died in 1956.

The inscription on Edith's gravestone reads, "They seek a country."

For twenty years on her own, and then for another twenty years with Victoria Hayward, Edith Watson saw more of Canada than perhaps any Canadian had before her, and few have since. No one knows exactly how many miles she travelled, but her journeys in Canada, stretched out in a line along the equator, would have gone around the world at least four times. Year after year she ventured into remote places, meeting the huge variety of people who make up the "Canadian mosaic," and recording it all with her camera. She has left us with a legacy of thousands of unique, historical photographs of the rural areas of the second-largest country on earth.

ALEXANDRA DAVID-NÉEL

1868–1969

ALEXANDRA DAVID-NÉEL was a born rebel and wanderer. She rebelled against the unloving way her parents treated her and each other, and also against society's expectations of how women were to live and work. She sought peace and a sense of belonging in the philosophy and practice of the Buddhist religion, and she felt more at home travelling the roads and mountains of India, China, and Tibet than she ever felt in her homes in Europe.

Alexandra David was born in Paris, France, in 1868. From a very early age, she wandered away from home—and on several occasions ran away—in search of adventure. In her teens she discovered Buddhism and decided to study it and to travel the areas where Buddhism was the main religion. In her early twenties, an inheritance allowed her to travel by sea to India and Ceylon, now known as Sri Lanka. She crisscrossed the two countries and finally, when her money ran out, returned to Paris.

For many people that trip would have been enough. For Alexandra it was just the beginning. But she needed money.

Europe in the 1890s was exciting and full of energy. For a young woman this meant more opportunities than ever before. Alexandra, who had won singing contests in her teens, became an opera singer. With the Opéra-Comique and then the Greek L'Opéra d'Athènes, she travelled throughout Europe and as far east as Hanoi. In the East she experienced a feeling she had not known before: she had come home. This was where she was meant to be.

In 1902 she became a director for the Casino de Tunis in northern Africa. There she met Philippe-François Néel, whom she married the next year. Their loyalty to one another lasted for the rest of their lives. But it was hardly an ordinary marriage. After only a few weeks together, the couple went their separate ways. They never lived together again.

Philippe suggested that if Alexandra wanted to travel, he would pay for her voyages and attend to business at home.

For eight years, Alexandra travelled Europe, making a few short trips to Tunis to visit Philippe. She also studied Buddhism and Sanskrit and lectured in comparative religion. But her real desire was to live philosophies, not read about and teach them. By 1911 she was ready to return to India. The plan was to go for

Although Alexandra and her husband only lived together for a few weeks, they were married for almost forty years. When he died, she said that she had lost "the best of husbands and my only friend."

a few months. She returned fourteen years later.

> The current Dalai Lama has been in exile from Tibet since 1959. Dharamasala, India, where he lives and which is close to the Tibetan border, is known as the "Little Lhasa."

In Calcutta, Alexandra established contacts that would be useful in her travels. She socialized with officials in the British Consulate and with the governor of Madras. She studied at the College of Sanskrit at the University of Calcutta, and in 1912 was the first Western woman to be granted an interview with the Dalai Lama. He was impressed by Alexandra, and encouraged her to learn the Tibetan language. She also met the Crown Prince of Sikkim, who became king in 1914. All the while she continued to study Buddhism. Her ability to learn languages, and her powerful acquaintances and friends, made it possible for Alexandra to go where few women, and often no European, had ever gone.

In 1912 she went to Sikkim and stayed in the royal temple. She was granted the title lamina (woman lama), and given a red lama's robe to wear. She visited villages and monasteries with the prince, and then continued her travels on her own. She went to remote areas with an interpreter and porters to carry camping gear. She went far enough north to reach the border of Tibet, high in the Himalayas. She passed glaciers, saw valleys filled with clouds, and stood in awe looking at the vast Tibetan plateau, "immense, void and resplendent under the luminous sky of Central Asia."

Back in Sikkim, she asked for a personal assistant to be assigned to her. Yongden, a fifteen-year-old monk who had arrived at the monastery at the age of eight, was chosen because of his yearning to travel. Alexandra and Yongden were together until Yongden's death.

World War I broke out in Europe in August 1914. It was

Alexandra and Yongden.

not a good time to try to return to France. Alexandra had no visa and so could not enter Tibet legally, but she smuggled herself and Yongden into Tibet anyway. There she first stayed in a monastery, then left Yongden at the monastery and moved even higher into the mountains, where she lived in a cave as a hermit in an area where some Buddhist nuns also lived. The nuns told her of a holy man in an even more remote area, and despite an injured shoulder she went to see him. He accepted her as a novice and she stayed near him for the winter. She spent most of her time alone, breaking her solitude only to meet with him.

She was snowed in part of the time. The cold was very hard on her. But the solitude, the quiet, and the closeness to nature gave her joy and fed her soul in a way she didn't even know she needed. She set her own schedule, she studied and hiked and meditated. Becoming a Buddhist hermit gave her a sense of being accepted for who she was in a way that life in Europe never had and never would. This bitter winter in a cave almost 4,000 meters (13,000 feet) up in the mountains was the happiest time of Alexandra's life.

The next year the government of India caught up with her, fined her, and deported her for having gone into Tibet illegally. That deportation order gave her the determination she needed to go to Lhasa, the Forbidden City, high in the mountains and the headquarters of Tibetan Buddhism. Since India would not let her go into Tibet, she decided to take the only other route she could: through China.

Alexandra and Yongden travelled through Burma, Japan, and Korea, before they reached China. They stayed in Peking for four months and then set out across the plains and mountains. China was in the middle of several civil wars, so the danger was a greater challenge than their difficult route. In August 1918, they arrived at the huge monastery of Kumbum (*kumbum* means "one hundred thousand Buddha images"), high in the mountains of Tibet (now in China). Women were not allowed to live in a monastery, but because of her standing as a Buddhist, her age, and the blessing of the Dalai Lama, Alexandra was given a small house on the edge of the grounds. There she studied and met pilgrims from all over Tibet. Since she was forbidden to attend some ceremonies, Yongden went to them and told her about them. She stayed there for almost three years.

She decided to continue her explorations and go to Lhasa. She knew about earlier expeditions to the city. Some travellers had made it to this fabled place; more had turned back or died because of the terrain, the cold, or the bandits. But Alexandra was determined.

Her travels over the next several years are not precisely known. We do know that her route was complicated because the wars in China often made it impossible to go directly from one place to another. She went to Lake Koko Nor and to Szechuan in China, then west toward Tibet. Soldiers then turned her to the north, to Mongolia and the Gobi Desert. She had no money and could rarely get letters out to Philippe. Starvation, exposure, and being shot at were constant dangers. She arranged with Yongden that if she did not survive, her young companion would get a message to her husband.

She carried a pistol, which she only shot once, and a whip, with which she took knives away from marauders. Her status as a Buddhist lama meant nothing in the Gobi

Desert. Once, when she was ordered to return the way she had come, she told the soldiers, "Give me my revolver, I shall kill myself. Everyone will then believe that you have murdered me and you will suffer the consequences of this crime." Eventually the soldiers begged her to go away quietly.

Alexandra and Yongden travelled south from the Gobi Desert to Chengtu, in Szechuan province. So that their destination could remain secret, they circled west and south. Seven months later they reached the border of Burma. To that point, the travel had been fairly ordinary. Now, at the end of October 1923, she stained her face with a mixture of cocoa and charcoal, darkened her hair with Chinese ink, braided it and lengthened it with black braids made from the hair of yaks, and put large hoop earrings in her ears. She then dressed as a Tibetan beggar in a heavy wool robe and backpack, and set out.

Alexandra and Yongden passed illegally from China into Tibet at the Dokar Pass high in the Kha Karpo mountains. No Westerner had been in this region before, and few have since. She climbed mountain after mountain, going through passes of up to 5,500 meters (18,000 feet). She and Yongden were almost buried in snow many times. Once they walked for nineteen hours without a break, and more than once they nearly starved. Occasionally they stayed overnight with a family in their tent and shared the food cooked in their fire. On they walked, through deep snow and biting cold and wind. Over and over they were advised not to do this and told that no woman could. "Not for one minute did I consider giving up the game. I had sworn that a woman could pass, and I would!"

The last stage of the journey went along a caravan route and all travellers had to obtain a pass. How was a Western woman to get one? When the time came, Yongden went into the house at the checkpoint, and Alexandra sat outside on a stone, chanting prayers. Yongden got the passes and no one paid any attention to Alexandra.

Lhasa, surrounded by hills, sits on a plain 3,600 meters (11,800 feet) high. The Monastery of Potala, the centre of Tibetan Buddhism and the palace fort of the Dalai Lama, rises above the city. The Potala has hundreds of rooms, with stairs and passages and gold-roofed pavilions, and it all seems to grow out of the rock it is built on.

Alexandra arrived in Lhasa in a sandstorm. The New Year's celebrations were taking place, so she was able to wander into the city with the thousands of pilgrims who were there for the holiday. She had changed her clothing so that she looked like someone from Ladakh in the far west of Tibet. She did this so that her accent would be mistaken for that of someone from a distant province. It worked. She mingled with the crowds, bargained and ate in the bazaar, and bought books. No one guessed that she was not Tibetan.

So far so good. But she wanted to get into the Potala, so

Alexandra (on yak) with a Sikkim escort on the way to Tibet.

> "All sights, all things which are Lhasa's own beauty and peculiarity, would have to be seen by the lone woman explorer who had the nerve to come to them from afar, the first of her sex."
>
> – Alexandra David-Néel

Yongden offered to act as a guide for two villagers who were in the city to sell barley. The three men went ahead, with Alexandra pretending to be an old, bent, peasant woman. Once again, no one noticed her. She went through the palace in awe of the hundreds of gold, silver, and copper images of Buddha. There were also silk prayer banners, jade carvings, and porcelain bowls and statues everywhere. There were other images too: the gods, animals, and demons of Bon, the religion of the area before Buddhism. She climbed to the top of the palace and looked out across the gold roofs to the plain and the mountains. She had done it: she was at the top of the Forbidden City of Lhasa.

Alexandra stayed in Lhasa for two months. Then she and Yongden left on horseback for India. Only when she was safe in Calcutta did she admit in a letter to Philippe that a young strong man might well have perished on that trip. For her, a slight woman of fifty-six, the journey had been particularly foolhardy.

Determined to settle down and repay Philippe's kindness and financial support, she wrote him that she was coming home. But he had long ago gotten used to life without her. Perhaps, he suggested, she would like to live in North America. Despite Philippe's lack of enthusiasm, in May 1925, fourteen years after her departure, Alexandra arrived in Europe.

She got to work writing books and articles on Buddhism, Tibetan society, her travels throughout the East, and her explorations in China and Tibet. She also went on speaking tours. The talks and books were hugely popular, and she became a celebrity and made quite a lot of money from her work. Then in 1927 she bought a house outside Nice, France, in Dignes-les-Bains, a little town with a river, fields of lavender, and a view of the mountains. She called her house Samten Dzong (Tibetan for "House of Meditation"). She continued working, and Philippe visited on occasion.

> "Some will think that I have been uncommonly lucky. I shall not disagree; but luck has a cause, like anything else, and I believe there exists a mental attitude capable of shaping circumstances more or less according to one's wishes."
>
> – Alexandra David-Néel

Ten years of quiet life in southern France was all Alexandra could take. At the beginning of 1936, at sixty-eight, she and Yongden took a train to Berlin and then Moscow, where they boarded the Trans-Siberian Railway to Vladivostok. She became a nomad again, travelling from Vladivostok through Manchuria and into China.

But the experience of travelling was not the same. The Japanese army was pushing south from Manchuria, the country was devastated, and food was hard to get. When she was in Chungking, Japanese planes bombed the airport. Westerners in China, no longer safe, were fleeing south to Hong Kong. But even if Alexandra could get to Hong Kong, she had no money to get back to France. She decided to go southwest toward Tibet. Violent rain continued for the entire time she and Yongden climbed in the mountains, soaking everyone and turning the roads to mud. The two of them reached Tatsienlu, in Tibet, shortly before her seventieth birthday.

Alexandra kept writing. Somehow she got manuscripts out to Philippe. The French ambassador told her to be ready to flee at a moment's notice. Then, with the Japanese bombardment of Chungking, no letters could get in or out.

By September 1939 she had finished one book and begun another. Chinese troops were fully mobilized and

Japanese bombs continued to be a threat. She mailed a letter to Philippe in July; he received it at the end of November. World War II had started, and he could not get any money for himself or for her. The good news was that her French publishing house, which had stopped operating, was working again by late 1940 and was going to reissue one of her books.

Philippe died in January 1941. Alexandra wrote, "I had lost the best of husbands, and my only friend."

France was occupied by the Nazis for four more years, so she could not go there. But in 1944, after six years of living in Tatsienlu, there was no choice but to flee the bombs and guns that were by then just outside the town. Alexandra and Yongden joined the other refugees to walk to the French Military Mission. Some days there was no food, but they kept going. The two refugees found the French officials where they were hiding, probably, although no one knows for sure, in Kunming. Alexandra then talked the diplomats into finding a plane to take her and Yongden and 400 kilograms (almost 900 pounds) of luggage to India. Alexandra was seventy-six.

In her house in France after the war, she continued to write and consult with scholars, other students of the East, and admirers of her explorations and writings. She arranged to leave her books and belongings to the town in exchange for no tax charges (there is now an institute in her honor in Dignes-les-Bains). Yongden died in 1955 at age fifty-five. After much looking, Alexandra found a new assistant and student who worked with her until she died at Samten Dzong in September 1969, seven weeks before her hundred-and-first birthday. At her request, her own and Yongden's ashes were placed into the Ganges River in India.

> "I was inspired by the desire to do something no one else had and to try myself physically and intellectually."
> — Alexandra David-Néel

After a lonely and unhappy childhood, Alexandra David-Néel managed to establish exactly the life that suited her. Her highly unusual marriage seems to have worked for both her and Philippe. She expertly interpreted Buddhism for Europeans and North Americans by writing tremendously popular articles and books, and she continued to write until seventeen days before her death. She became a Tibetan lama, learned to speak the Tibetan language like a native, and travelled to places that were so remote that, to this day, there are no accurate maps of them. This is what she is most remembered for: that she explored vast areas of Asia where few, if any, Westerners—and no Western woman—had ever gone.

PHYLLIS MUNDAY

1894–1990

PHYLLIS JAMES MUNDAY, the great mountaineer and explorer, was the first woman to climb Mount Robson, at the time believed to be the highest peak in Canada.

Phyllis had her first big adventure in 1901, when she was seven years old. Her family moved from Ceylon, now Sri Lanka, to Canada. They stayed first in Manitoba, and then moved to Nelson, British Columbia. It must have been quite a shock to go from a hot country where the busy household included servants and a nanny for each child, to a small log house in Nelson where there were few neighbors or friends.

After five years in Nelson, the family moved to Vancouver. Her father wanted Phyllis to be a tennis champion, but the mountains called to her. She started close to home, with Grouse Mountain on Vancouver's north shore, a three-hour climb. When she was sixteen, she climbed the Lions, the 1,646-meter (5,400-foot) peaks that hover just to the north of Vancouver. There would be no tennis player in the James family.

In 1910 Phyllis asked her mother to form a Girl Scout troop. There were Boy Scouts, why not scouting for girls? Girl Guides had just been founded in England—after Lord and Lady Baden-Powell realized that more than 8,000 girls had joined the Boy Scouts! The girls had used the ploy that women have long used to be accepted in places that would not allow women: they had enrolled using their initials rather than their first names. In Canada, the scouting movement for girls was called Girl Guides soon after the troop was founded, and Phyl (as her friends called her) remained active with the Guides as long as her health allowed. She established groups for girls in remote areas, she taught climbing, camping, and nature lore, and she held every possible position in the organization. She was the only mountaineer in North America to be awarded Guiding's highest honor, the Bronze Cross, after she spent three weeks on Grouse Mountain caring for a head-injured climber who could not be moved. In many ways, Phyllis established Girl Guides in British Columbia.

Phyllis James's father wanted her to be a tennis champion. She told him that she wanted to climb mountains instead. When he said to her, "You've climbed one mountain, why do you want to climb more?" she reminded him that he'd played more than one game of tennis.

When World War I began in Europe in 1914, Phyllis trained with St. John's Ambulance, got a job in the Military Annex of the New

Westminster General Hospital, and served with the Voluntary Detachment. In 1918 she met Don Munday, a twenty-eight-year-old soldier and mountaineer who was recovering from war injuries. Phyllis didn't like Don much at first, but he was quiet, polite, and a climber. Over the next year they climbed two mountains and got to know each other and she changed her mind about him. In February 1920, Phyl and Don married and fled their wedding reception to go climbing. Their honeymoon was a week on Grouse Mountain.

Phyllis and Don began to explore the high peaks around Mount Robson. Phyllis's climbs in 1920 included Lynx Mountain and the north ridge of Mount Resplendent. Her ambition, though, was to climb Mount Robson, the highest peak in North America.

The couple lived on Grouse Mountain in a tent while they built the log cabin that was to be their home. On March 26, 1921, their daughter Edith was born. Edith's mountain climbing experiences began when she was eleven weeks old. Phyllis carried her newborn in a pack she had made. In their camps, an oven door served as a cradle, and by all reports, Edith was quite happy with the arrangement.

Until Edith was three, Phyllis and Don's trips were relatively close to home. Then in 1924, four years after her first trip to the Mount Robson area, Phyllis was back at Robson Pass. After some smaller climbs, it was time to try to reach the summit of Robson itself.

The climbing party included seven men and two women, Phyllis and Annette Buck. It was a longstanding practice not to allow women to go beyond the timberline, but this time was different. The group carried with them three tents, a stove, food, and bedding. At 1,850 meters (about 6,000 feet), they encountered the danger of a major avalanche. Then a guide fell through a snow bridge. The climbers were able to save him, and the climb continued. The ice sloped at forty-five-degree angles, and huge blocks of ice rose in the climbers' way. The crew spent the night on the slope, and late the next afternoon, Phyllis James Munday became the first woman to stand on the top of Mount Robson. After taking overnight shelter huddled under rocks at the summit, the climbers returned to base camp.

The thrill of climbing the highest peak in North America was huge. But while she was nearing and then at the top of Robson, Phyllis began to look around at the surrounding peaks, seeing the mountains from a height few had ever reached ... she saw ... she wondered ... did she see ... a higher mountain? Everyone knew, had known for a long time, that Robson was the pinnacle. But was it? What mountain was that off in the distance, anyway? How high was it? No one knew anything about this "new" mountain Phyllis had found. She called it Mystery Mountain.

The next summer, Phyllis was with the third group ever to explore the Premier Range of the Cariboo Mountains, west of Mount Robson. She participated in the first ascent of Mount Sir John Thompson and the second climb of Mount Sir Wilfrid Laurier, the highest peak in the Cariboos. She also went to Lake O'Hara and climbed mounts Hungabee and Victoria. In the course of these climbs she became convinced that Mystery Mountain probably was higher than Robson. She began serious plans to climb her mysterious mountain.

The Coast Mountains, "a formidable, savage range," run parallel to the Pacific Ocean for 1,500 kilometers (nearly 1,000 miles) north from Vancouver. The climate in these mountains makes them, even now, almost impassable. Frequent heavy rain, furious and unpredictable rivers, and undergrowth below the treeline makes even walking almost impossible and prevents the building of any permanent roads or paths. Where only a few of the Rockies have a vertical rise of more than 1,800 meters (about 5,900 feet), the tightly packed Coast Mountains consistently rise vertically more than 3,000 meters (almost 10,000 feet). Mystery Mountain is one of these mountains.

Over the next twelve years Phyllis made sixteen attempts to climb Mystery Mountain. She approached it from every possible angle. In 1926 Phyllis and Don's daughter Edith stayed with a family at a logging camp on Bute Inlet while her parents and their expedition climbed. After thirteen days they were only forty-eight kilometers (thirty miles) from their starting point and 100 meters (over 300 feet) above sea level. Don estimated that, because they had to return to base camp so many times to move their equipment and supplies, each person covered over 160 kilometers (100 miles) relaying supplies in three trips. Ultimately the undergrowth defeated them, and they turned back.

Phyllis and Don climbing beside a river.

In July 1927, Phyllis's sister went with them. When the camp was hit by lightning, they gave up for the year. Also in 1927, the National Geographic Survey confirmed what Phyllis had suspected: Mystery Mountain, which they now named Mount Waddington, was 4,015 meters (over 13,000 feet) high and was in fact higher than the famous Mount Robson.

In 1928 Phyllis and her

expedition tried again to climb Mount Waddington. Again they had to turn back.

Her next attempt was in 1933. The climbing party—six climbers, three guides, and seventeen horses—tried to approach Waddington from the northeast. This route went across Scimitar Glacier and through swamps, thickets, rockslides, and raging creeks. Trees that had fallen in a forest fire blocked the way. It took five days to cut five kilometers (three miles) of trail through the canyon. The climbers cut stairs into the ice so the horses could climb. After three weeks of incredible effort, they decided that it was impossible to get to Mount Waddington from where they were. They turned to Mount Combatant, 3,701 meters (12,000 feet) high, and on July 14 made the first recorded climb of that peak, despite high winds that destroyed much of their equipment. Again Phyllis and the others had made mountaineering history, and yet again they had been defeated in the climb they really wanted to make.

A year later they went as close to Mount Waddington as they could by sea. Once bad weather made them turn back, and a second time difficulty with defective climbing equipment (spikes and rope) turned them back. They climbed Finality Mountain, 2,833 meters (9,300 feet) high, then returned to Vancouver until they could make yet another attempt to reach the top of Mount Waddington the next year.

In the summer of 1935 floods forced them to turn back. So Phyllis, Don, and Edith explored up the coast in a boat they had built, the *Edidonphyl*, which Edith had named for the three of them.

Other climbers made it to the top of Mount Waddington in July 1936. But Phyllis and Don didn't let that stop them. This time they took wire, clothesline, pulleys, and a seat harness to get them across flooding rivers. At a canyon on the edge of Kliniklini Glacier they saw a grizzly bear and stopped to watch it and take pictures. What they didn't realize was that a mother grizzly with her two cubs was about to charge them from behind. When they did see her, they waved their hands and yelled and the bear backed off. Then she changed her mind and charged Phyl. Don yelled, and he and the bear had a shouting match. The bear was better at it than he was, so he had to back off, but in doing so he fell onto a shelf of rock partway down the canyon. Now it was Phyl's turn to try to protect him. She grabbed an ice-axe, ready to attack. The bear turned and walked away.

Phyllis (left) climbing a glacier with an ice-axe.

Yet again Phyllis made the first recorded climbs of two mountains, often leading the group in dangerous crossings of rivers and inlets. By this time she was winning praise, recognition, and awards for her skill. She enjoyed all this. But she still had not accomplished her biggest dream. In her total of sixteen attempts, she once got to the northwest peak of Mount Waddington, and another time made it to within eighteen meters (sixty feet) of the summit. But as it turned out, Phyllis would never reach the top of her beloved "Mystery Mountain."

Many people climb mountains, but not all climbers also explore the mountains they climb. During their adventures, Phyllis and Don did a lot more than climb mountains. They noted the effects of high altitudes, difficult climbing for long periods, cold, and sometimes hunger on their fellow climbers. Phyllis noted the hallucinations that sometimes occurred, using one of her own as an illustration: she had at one time believed that she was on a tropical beach, when in fact she was standing on a glacier. She and Don collected samples and made careful observations of rocks, plants, and insects on their climbs. Phyllis also took photographs, many of which geologists and cartographers still use.

Winters were busy times, too. Phyllis made jams to take with them for energy and experimented with drying different foods. She baked bannock and collected other supplies for the trip, including beans, rice, biscuits, chocolate, nuts, and raisins. She made and repaired equipment, including the cotton bags for food, which she waterproofed by dipping them into melted tallow (an animal fat also used to make candles). She made a stove and stovepipe of old biscuit tins for the shack they used for two years, and added a homey touch by making curtains out of bandages. She and Don made down sleeping bags, a three-person, sail-silk tent that weighed less than two kilograms (four-and-a-half pounds), light, convenient custom backpacks, and lamps made out of empty powdered-milk cans.

By the mid-1930s Phyllis had developed arthritis. Even though she wrapped her knees in cold compresses at night, she was often in pain. In 1937 the family took the *Edidonphyl* 600 kilometers (about 370 miles) north of Vancouver through the most amazing countryside Phyl had ever seen to Bella Coola. From there they searched for Mount Stupendous, a peak they had seen during their climbs on Mount Waddington. All three family members then made the first recorded climb of the 2,728-meter (nearly 9,000-foot) mountain. Edith was sixteen, and this was her first major climb.

Mountain climbers have to be ready for anything. In

1938 "anything" included a forest fire near Bella Coola, which Phyl, Don, and Edith worked with firefighters to put out. Since women could not be on the firefighters' payroll, Phyl and Edith listed only their first initials and got paid the same $8 for their work as the men did.

When World War II broke out in 1939, Don was too old for the army, so he worked on the Vancouver docks and later taught skiing and climbing to troops. Phyllis led expeditions for the Alpine Club of Canada.

After the war, they returned to making still more first recorded climbs. Don did his last climbing in the late fall of 1949. By Christmas he was seriously ill, and he died the next June. He was 59 and Phyllis was 55. Later that year Phyl dropped some of his ashes, wrapped in his favorite climbing hat, from a plane over Mount Munday, named for the famous pair. The rest she scattered in Garibaldi Park.

Phyl continued to climb, but did not try Mount Waddington again. In 1955 she flew over it with Sir Edmund Hillary, the first European person known to have reached the top of Mount Everest. And in 1982, when she said in an interview with CTV that she would like to make a final visit to Mount Waddington, the network granted her wish and flew her over the mountain she had explored so thoroughly. It had been fifty-six years since her first trip.

At eighty-eight, Phyllis was still doing walks and advocating exploring mountains rather than simply climbing them. The difference? To a mountaineer, the climb, the accomplishment, is everything. An explorer also takes into account the landscape and everything that is in it—she sees, smells, tastes, and lives with the mountains she climbs. An explorer, as Phyllis said, has "reverence for it all, love for it all, adoration for it."

In 1987, Natalie Renner became the youngest Canadian to climb Mount Assiniboine, the highest peak in the southern Rockies. She was nine years old.

In 2003, seven years and forty-nine days after she began, Nancy Hansen became the first woman to climb all fifty-four of the 3,354-meter (11,000-foot) peaks in the Rockies. Five men who also climbed them all each took over twenty years. Nancy climbed a total of 119,394 vertical meters (more than 390,000 feet).

Phyllis Munday was a member of the B.C. Mountaineering Club and had joined the Alpine Club of Canada in 1920. She belonged to six other outdoor and climbing clubs in three countries and is the only person to have been honored by three international climbing clubs. From 1953 to 1969, she edited *Canadian Alpine Journal*. In 1973 she was made a member of the Order of Canada and granted an honorary doctorate from the University of Victoria. In 1998, Canada Post/Postes Canada issued its Legendary Canadians series of stamps. She was the only woman honored in the series.

Phyllis had photographed and developed geographical and botanical prints since late 1920s. She filmed some of her climbs, lectured, and presented exhibits about mountains and mountain climbing, and the flowers and animals of the mountains. She taught mountain first aid. And she trained many people in ice and snow climbing.

Phyllis James Munday climbed a hundred mountains. A third of that number were first known ascents; many more were the first known climbs by a woman. She discovered the highest peak in Canada. That she never got to the top of Mount Waddington doesn't seem, in the end, to have bothered her: "We went in ... to find out all we possibly could about glaciers and mountains and animals and nature and everything about that particular area—completely unknown before we went into it—so that we could bring out the information for the interest of other people as well as ourselves." Phyl's long, full life ended in April 1990, her ninety-sixth year.

FREYA STARK

1893–1993

FREYA STARK SET OUT BY HERSELF to go to sea in 1896. She was turned back that time—she was three years old—but it wasn't long before her travelling life began.

Freya was born in Paris, France, in 1893, where her parents were both painters. The family soon moved to her father's home in England, where they stayed until Freya was ten. That summer she went with her Italian mother Flora and younger sister Vera to Dronero, Italy. They stayed for sixteen years, until the end of World War I. By that time, the Starks' marriage had ended, and Freya's father had gone to live in British Columbia on the west coast of Canada.

Life in Italy was difficult. Money was frequently scarce

and her mother's reputation for flirting with men made things awkward more than once. Freya's health was not good. She had heart trouble and was often confined to bed with fevers and pneumonia. To make things worse, when she was thirteen, during a visit to the carpet factory her mother co-owned, Freya's hair was caught in the steel shaft of a mechanical loom. It twirled her round and round, pulling at her hair and slamming her legs against the walls. By the time the machine could be stopped, her hair and much of her scalp had been ripped from her head. She spent four months in hospital and was self-conscious about her scars for the rest of her life. But even when she was confined to bed, Freya read about faraway places and studied the languages she would use later in her travels.

After her accident Freya was self-conscious about her looks. She usually pulled her hair across part of her face to cover the scars and wore hats much of the time.

In 1912 Freya left her family in Italy to study history at the University of London. When World War I broke out two years later, she returned to Italy and spent the war working as a nurse and censor of the mail. At the end of the war in 1919, she started making serious travel plans, which included finding the money she needed to support herself on the road.

The Islamic countries of the Near East and Arabia had captured Freya's imagination, and she decided to learn Arabic. She found a monk who had lived for thirty years in Beirut, and who had retired to San Remo, Italy, to raise Angora rabbits. Twice a week she walked for an hour, caught the train, and then walked two more miles to where he was living. Within months she was reading the K'oran in the original Arabic. While she was doing this, her income also rose: against the advice of her banker, she sank all her money into shares in the Canadian Grand Trunk Railway.

When Freya was a young woman, she made a large commission by smuggling a valuable painting from France into Italy. She turned down later opportunities to smuggle other objects, but admitted that "The art of smuggling ... has a spice of danger of its own."

The investment paid off, and she had enough money to travel. Her major journeys occurred from 1927 to 1933 in Lebanon, Iraq, and Iran, from 1935 to 1938 in southern Arabia, and from 1951 to 1965 in Greece, Turkey, and the Near East. After that, in her seventies and eighties, Freya made trips to China, Nepal, back to the Euphrates River, and in 1982, back again to the Himalayas.

In November 1927 Freya left for Lebanon. A month later she was living in a room in Brummana, where the men stared at her, children followed her through the streets, and women watched her from their houses. She learned to relax and take things as they came, studied Arabic, and spoke with anyone who would talk to her. She found that by being relaxed and unhurried she could move easily in this new place. She was happy.

Then she went into the desert. It was an enchanting experience. She wrote to a friend, "Yesterday was a wonderful day: for I discovered the Desert! ... Camels appeared on our left hand: first a few here and there, then more and more, until the whole herd came browsing along, five hundred or more ... Their huge legs rose up all around me like columns ... I never imagined that my first sight of the desert would come as such a shock of beauty and enslave me right away."

After seven months, she went back to Europe, knowing that her life had changed forever. She didn't yet know what that meant, but she did know that any plans for an ordinary life in the north of Italy—or anywhere else—were gone.

In 1929 Freya Stark moved to Baghdad, in Iraq, a very different Baghdad from the one we now see on the news.

Eight years earlier Iraq had gone from being a British colony to having a monarchy of its own. Many British and other European people still lived there, most of them in a very wealthy area where few Iraqis went. Freya did not want to be apart from the people whose country she was living in. She moved into a room in the home of a shoemaker and his family, ate with them, socialized with them, and practised speaking Arabic.

From that base Freya made several exploratory journeys to Iraq and Persia (now called Iran). Many of these trips were to places other foreigners had gone, but from 1930 to 1933, she made serious explorations in Persia. The first trip was to the area called Luristan, in the Zagros Mountains. Little was known of this area or its people, and no maps of it existed. The nomadic people of Luristan, the Lurs, had at that time almost no contact with the outside world. Over several weeks, Freya climbed the mountains and valleys of the Zagros on horseback. She visited and photographed the Lurs, getting to know them in a way very few outsiders ever had or would, for their culture would soon be changed forever by contact with outsiders.

Freya heard about a treasure trove of gold coins, statues, and jewels that was said to be hidden in a cave near the city of Nihavend and went with a guide to look for the fortune. At one point she broke away from her escort and went exploring on her own. The Baghdad police, having heard of the treasure-hunting and the expedition, followed her. When her guide did not meet her where they had arranged, she decided that the police must have discovered their plans and decided to let the treasure go.

"I have found that one can nearly always do what one sets out for, if it is only one thing at a time."

— Freya Stark

Next Freya went looking for the ruins of castles. Again she went high into the mountains, this time to Mazanderan at the south end of the Caspian Sea. Tales of the castles, ancient myths, and what she called "a lovely blank on the map" all called her there. Along the way she became very ill with dysentery and malaria. Without the help of a local woman who took her in and cared for her, she would have died. But this didn't stop her. Her explorations of the Elburz Mountains and Mazanderan and the mapping she did of the area gained her recognition from the Royal Geographical Society, the Royal Asiatic Society, and the British government. After almost three years, she returned to London in the summer of 1933.

The publication of her first two books contributed to Freya's growing fame. She was able to draw together the landscape, people, history, and culture of the areas she explored in a fascinating way that few other people could. Her writing was colorful, dignified, and respectful of the peoples and cultures she had met. Her books sold extremely well. She was in demand as a speaker, and many people,

Freya, at right, and two companions on a picnic in the desert, Egypt, 1942.

> "I wanted space, distance, history and danger, and I was interested in the living world."
>
> — Freya Stark

including some influential members of large organizations, became interested in her travels. All of this meant that she could now earn her living with her explorations.

She set out again in 1935. This time she took a ship first to Aden, then to the south coast of Arabia. She was headed for Shabwa in the Hadramaut, a district in Yemen. It was a seven-day donkey ride with no water along the way. No European had ever been there before.

Shibam, called the "skyscraper town of the desert" because of its tall buildings made from mud bricks, was to have been the starting point of her journey to Shabwa. But Freya became desperately sick with measles, which at that time was a very serious illness for children and adults alike. Combined with the malaria and dysentery of her earlier trip, the measles affected her heart, which had never been strong. Again she thought she would die. Instead of going to Shabwa, she was airlifted to a hospital in Aden. She survived, and turned her disappointment at her missed adventure into another best-selling book.

On her next trip, Freya joined an archaeological expedition to Yemen. Her major discovery on that trip was that she was no archaeologist. She wanted to visit with the people and learn their history and their ways, not gather pieces of old pottery from the dirt. Those pieces might talk to researchers, she decided, but they didn't speak to her. At the end of the dig, Freya decided to make a final trip through Arabia to locate ports in Cana. These ports were known to exist, but Europeans did not know their exact locations. Sick yet again, she kept going and rode almost 200 kilometers (120 miles) by camel in the boiling sun. At a town a short distance from her destination, she was advised that the rest of the trip was extremely dangerous because of frequent attacks by bandits, so she joined a heavily armed caravan of twenty-seven camels which was carrying a load of tobacco. Also part of the caravan were four relatives of the sultan and twelve bodyguards.

Freya Stark's experiences in Arabia and Persia established her as an explorer, historian, observer of cultures, and a very successful writer. During World War II, between 1939 and 1945, she worked for the British government in Egypt, Iraq, and Arabia to build support for the British war efforts among the Arab nations. In 1947 she married Stewart Perowne, a good friend with whom she had worked closely during the war, but they both quickly discovered that they were meant to be friends and not spouses, and divorced four years later.

In 1951 Freya was fifty-eight years old, an age when many people assumed that her travelling days would be almost over. Instead, for the next fourteen years she travelled extensively in Greece, Turkey, and Syria. She liked the Mediterranean, but she fell in love with Turkey. For centuries Turkey had been where East met West. Trade and travel between Asia and Europe had passed through there, empires had risen and fallen there, and religions mingled there. Freya visited Turkey over and over. She followed the trail Alexander the Great had taken through that area in 334 BCE. She looked for hidden villages, peoples not known to the wider world, and landscapes both forbidding and enchanting. In these years she also learned the Turkish language and published more than ten new books.

In her seventies, Freya went to China for the first time. At seventy-six, she toured remote sections of Afghanistan by

"Curiosity ought to increase as one gets older." — Freya Stark

Freya, at right (in hat), crossing a river in the Himalayas on a donkey, 1970.

Jeep. Two years later she explored Nepal, high in the Himalayas, on a pony. In 1977, when she was eighty-four, the BBC television network filmed her on a slowly sinking raft on the Euphrates River. At eighty-nine she rode a donkey to the base of Annapurna, in the Himalayas. This, too, was filmed, and it worried some of the film crew that Freya was so stiff after riding the donkey that she had to be lifted down from it and carried to her tent. She was fine, however, and the filming continued.

In 1963, the year she turned seventy, Freya had bought a little rundown cottage in Asolo, Italy, near where she had grown up. In Asolo, she wrote books, greeted friends, fixed up her house, and prepared for the next trip. During this time honors poured in, and in 1972 she was made a Dame of the British Empire, the equivalent, for a woman, of knighthood.

In May 1984, she was presented with the key to the town of Asolo in a ceremony with much pomp, music, and color. This was to be her last public appearance. Dame Freya Stark died at her home on May 9, 1993, at one hundred years of age.

ADA BLACKJACK

1898–1983

BY THE TIME SHE WAS TWENTY-FIVE, Ada Blackjack was a reluctant hero. For months she had kept herself alive, alone, on an uninhabited island north of Siberia. For months before that, she had taken care of one of the men who lay dying in their cabin after the other three members of the expedition had gone for help. When, starved and dazed, she stepped onto the mainland at Nome, Alaska, in September 1923, she was thirty pounds lighter than she had been when she left. And although she didn't know it at the time, of the five people who journeyed to Wrangel Island two years earlier, she was the only one still alive.

Ada never wanted to be a hero. She didn't even want to be an explorer. She wanted a quiet, private life. But sometimes life has surprises in mind for us ...

Ada was born in 1898 in Spruce Creek, an Inuit community outside Solomon, Alaska. When she was eight years old, Ada's mother sent her to school in Nome. She learned to speak, read, and write English, and to cook, sew, and clean in the manner of the Methodist missionaries who taught her. She never really learned the skills of her own people: how to trap, build shelters, and live with a large family and tribal community.

Ada married a violent man, Jack Blackjack, and for five years he beat her and her three children. When he finally left her, two of the children had died, and she and her son Bennett were stranded in the wilderness of the Seward Peninsula. She walked the forty miles to Nome, carrying Bennett, who had tuberculosis, much of the way. She was twenty-one.

In Nome, Ada sewed and cleaned houses, but there was not enough work and the pay was so poor that she could not buy Bennett's medications. Hard as it was for her to do, she took him to an orphanage where he would be cared for. She visited him as often as she could, but there was little more that she could do for him.

Vilhjalmur Stefansson called himself a Scandinavian explorer because he thought that made him more interesting than who he really was: William Stephenson from Manitoba. Stefansson somehow became interested in Wrangel Island, in the Arctic Ocean north of Siberia. He decided to claim the island for Canada, or if Canada didn't want it, for Britain. Wrangel, he believed, would make a strategic site for an airport north of Russia, which by the early 1920s had become a Communist country, the Union of Soviet Socialist Republics. Had he done his research,

Stefansson would have known that neither Britain nor Canada wanted the island and that Russia had claimed it a hundred years earlier without any argument from any other country. But since he did not check it out, the facts didn't stop him, and he went ahead with his plan to place people and the British and/or Canadian flag on the uninhabited island. First, he set out to form an expedition.

The four men Stefansson hired could hardly have been worse choices for Arctic survival. He wanted a university graduate to lead the group, so he picked Allan Crawford, age twenty, who had just graduated from the University of Toronto and had never been north of Toronto in his life. Second in command, and really the leader, was Lorne Knight, twenty-eight, who was actually one of the very few survivors of an earlier expedition to Wrangel Island. Fred Maurer, also twenty-eight, had been north before as well. And Milton Galle, who was nineteen years old, fell in love with Stefansson's descriptions of "the friendly north" and asked to be included. Galle had never been away from his home in New Braunfels, Texas.

The four men arrived in Nome in the spring of 1921. Stefansson had sent their supplies and equipment, including 2,250 kilograms (5,000 pounds) of food in addition to guns, traps, harpoons, ammunition, clothing, cooking gear, coffee, tea, chewing gum, and at Galle's request, twenty-six boxes of candy. In Nome they advertised for Inuit to accompany them in order to sew the rest of the clothing they would need and help hunt for food along the way. The pay would be $50 a month for two years. When a friend told Ada about the opportunity, she realized that the

Because Ada left home very young and was brought up in a town, she never learned the traditional survival skills of hunting, cooking, building a shelter. She was totally unprepared to survive on Wrangel Island and learned what she needed in order to stay alive.

money would be enough to get Bennett back and take care of them both for a while.

The expedition hired several Inuit families. When it came time to leave, Ada was the only person who showed up. All the others had decided the trip was too dangerous. Not sure whether she wanted to be the only woman on the expedition, she consulted a friend who had been on another of Stefansson's expeditions. Her friend knew Lorne Knight and she told Ada that he was a good man, would treat her well, and that she would be all right.

They left on September 9, 1921. The next day the ship, the *Silver Wave*, stopped at East Cape, Siberia. Once again, the men tried to hire Inuit families to go along. Once again, everyone thought the trip too dangerous. The group collected more supplies and set out.

Six days later, after navigating vicious storms in which three of the four men were horribly seasick, the ship's crew put Ada and the four men ashore on Wrangel Island. Things

The expedition: Allan Crawford, Lorne Knight, Fred Maurer, and Milton Galle, holding Victoria, the "expedition cat." Ada is front and center.

looked good at first: the weather was mild, the sun warm, and the breeze gentle. There were even some flowers. And there were lots of animal tracks and driftwood for food and fires. All five expedition members were optimistic about the year they would spend there, at the end of which a ship would pick them up.

East Cape, Siberia, the easternmost point in Asia, is also the first land after the International Dateline, so it is the first place on earth to start each new day. It is sometimes called "The Place Where Time Begins."

They set about collecting wood, building shelter, making a table and chairs, and setting up their meteorological instruments. Ada made hoods for the parkas and sewed them on, did other sewing, began to knit mittens, and cooked for the group.

None of these people had ever fired a gun before. The guns terrified Ada, and she refused to shoot. Meanwhile, the first walrus the men tried to shoot slept unconcerned while their shells dropped around it.

The easy time was short-lived. Snow started falling on September 20, the temperature fell to minus 17.5 degrees Fahrenheit, and the ice started to close in. The sea froze flat and white. By mid-November the dark that would last for sixty-one days had descended.

Ada suffered from what is known as "Arctic hysteria," a condition that befalls many people who are trapped in a cold place of endless day or night. The person frightens easily, often runs away to try to find relief from the cold and the light or dark, cries, moans, and becomes sluggish. Some people commit suicide. Ada became desperately afraid. One day,

Milton Galle with Victoria.

when Lorne Knight was sharpening his knife, she fled onto the ice, certain that he was going to kill her. She ran and ran, and it took the men several hours to find her. They took her back to camp and tied her up so that she wouldn't run out and freeze to death. Fortunately for Ada, as often happens with people who get Arctic hysteria, one day in mid-December the terror was gone, and she was able to get on with her work as if nothing had happened.

By January 25, Wrangel Island had light for four hours a day. The temperature continued at around minus 40 degrees (the temperature where the Fahrenheit and Centigrade scales meet). The ship was to come in June or July. The plan was to send Ada home on it, even though the men had grown fond of her and would miss her.

June 2, despite the long periods of summer light, was the worst day so far, with blinding snow, a gale-force wind, and almost no food. But the ship would be there soon.

Meanwhile, Stefansson, who had stayed comfortably in Canada, had raised no money and found no ship. The families of the men on Wrangel Island were desperately begging him to send supplies and check to see if Ada and the men were all right. Finally he got a ship, the *Teddy Bear*, which left on August 20. With any luck the ship and the five people on the island would be back in Nome in two weeks.

But there was no luck. In late August, the Bering Strait and the Arctic Ocean had the worst ice and snow conditions in twenty-five years. The propeller of the *Teddy Bear* was damaged. It was too dangerous to keep going, and if the ship remained where it was, the ice would certainly trap it in mid-ocean, endangering both the ship

Wrangel Island still belongs to Russia. In the 1940s and 1950s it was sometimes used to train Soviet troops and secret agents. It now has a weather station with a handful of residents. No other country has ever showed interest in claiming it.

and everyone on it. On September 25, the *Teddy Bear* gave up and turned back. Stefansson, in his usual unrealistic manner, told the families: "There is no more need to worry about them than if they were in some European City ... They are just as likely as you or I in Texas or New York to be safe and well a year from now."

The reality was grim. Knight was having joint pain and could hardly walk. In mid-August, the expedition ran out of tea and sugar and started to ration bread. The normal cycle in the Arctic is for animals to move from one area to another. The animals that had been so plentiful for the first months had now all but disappeared. By the end of September, the sea was again frozen as far as they could see. There would be no ship that year. In November the firewood ran out and they moved their camp to an area where wood was available. Soon Ada and the men were living on nothing but walrus skin and decreased bread rations.

On January 7, 1923, Crawford and Knight set out to cross Siberia and get to Nome for help. The journey would take sixty to seventy days. Within two weeks they were back, exhausted, frostbitten, and blistered with cold. Crawford's feet and fingers had turned black, and Knight was very sick.

The expedition members faced some terrible decisions. If everyone stayed there they would all die. If some of them went for help, they still might all die. They decided that Crawford, Maurer, and Galle would go for help, leaving Ada and the ailing Lorne Knight to take care of each other. What Ada knew that the others didn't was that Knight had scurvy, a deficiency of vitamin C that is easily curable with fresh meat or fruits, especially citrus. Without fresh food, the disease would progress until he died. She would take the best care she could of him, but fruit was impossible, and unless they could get large quantities of fresh meat, she was being left to care for a dying man.

Maurer, Galle, and Crawford left on January 29. The next day there was a ferocious storm that trapped Ada, Lorne Knight, and Victoria, the expedition cat, in the cabin they had built from ice at the new camp. The cat slept, Lorne Knight read, and Ada knitted mittens. How the other three were doing out in the storm, they would never find out.

The days dragged on. There was almost no food. Ada, still terrified of guns, taught herself to shoot. Finally, at the end of February, she shot a fox. Other animals followed. But Knight was getting sicker and sicker. By this time he couldn't swallow or stand up, and he could barely speak. Ada was also weak. By May Knight's face was blue and his nose was bleeding all the time. Ada built a platform to watch for birds and bears she could shoot for food. Knight got to the point where he could not get out of his sleeping bag. One symptom of scurvy is that a person bleeds very easily, from the nose, skin, lungs, digestive tract—anywhere. If Knight moved he would bleed, so he tried to stay as still as possible.

He asked Ada to organize his papers and his trunk and make sure his rifle and camera got to his family. He gave her his family Bible. And he asked for a grave that would not be ransacked by animals or humans. Ada wrote in her journal, "I must stay alive. I will live."

Lorne Knight died on June 26. It was impossible to bury him, so Ada arranged his body and kept it in the cabin. She was now alone with Victoria, the cat. On June 28 she killed her first seal. She made a small skin boat for fishing, but she used it just twice before it blew out to sea. She made new soles for her boots, knit new fingers for her gloves, and started to work on a

> "There, with only a dead man as companion, surrounded by seas of ice, Ada Blackjack wrote the real epic of the North."
> *The World Magazine*, October 30, 1927

Ada and a polar bear.

parka she would need if she had to stay another winter on the island. It was getting later and later in the season. Would a boat come? On August 2 she shot five birds. The next day she found some greens and ate them. A week later, a bear raided her supplies and ate all her lard and seal blubber. On August 16 she noted that the ice was beginning to come in again. She had done what she could for Lorne Knight. Now she was doing her best to keep herself and the cat alive. It was time to prepare for winter.

Stefansson, meanwhile, had decided to quit the exploration business. He had no money and the British and Canadian governments would not give him enough to send a ship to pick up the members of the expedition. Russia was far from pleased at the potential claim to Wrangel Island, and the Canadian and British governments did not want to hear from this man who had made so much trouble. Then, even though it wasn't his to sell, Stefansson tried to sell Wrangel Island to a friend, who didn't want it. Again the families of the expedition members demanded that he send a ship, and finally he organized one to go.

The ship left on August 2. This time it reached the island. Where the captain had expected to find a camp there was no sign of life. Ten miles further along the shore they found the abandoned first camp. The ship's whistle blew, hoping for a response. There was none. Fog made any search impossible. Then, on the morning of August 20, through the fog, they saw a figure on the shore. The ship's captain, Harold Noice, climbed into a skin boat with several Inuit and went ashore. Ada asked where Crawford, Galle, and Maurer were. Noice told her that he had expected to find them on Wrangel Island. She told him she was there alone and asked if Noice would take her back to Nome. When he said of course, Ada collapsed on the shore.

Noice took her to the ship and went back with some men to bury Knight and get Victoria. The worst was over.

For years afterwards, battles raged over the records of the trip and the rights to the story. Noice and Stefansson fought with each other and the families of the men who were desperate to find out the fate of their loved ones. Reporters were everywhere, trying to get all the details.

Ada granted no interviews and spoke only a few words

Shortly before the rescue boat took her away for good, Ada was photographed standing by the grave of Lorne Knight, who was buried on Wrangel Island.

> "Brave? I don't know about that. But I would never give up hope while I'm still alive."
>
> – Ada Blackjack

to any reporters. The only interview she ever gave was in 1973, when she was seventy-four, a year after her son Bennett's death at fifty-eight. Over the years, she met with Crawford, Maurer, and Galle's families and told them what she could about the expedition and the sons, brothers, and husband who had disappeared. Rumor had it that they'd been seen on the Siberian shore in 1922. Perhaps they had died in a Russian prison, maybe they were living somewhere in Siberia. What seems most likely is that they perished in that first storm, just a day or two away from the camp, where Knight and Ada waited in vain. That mystery has never been solved.

Ada removed Bennett from the orphanage and took him to see doctors in Seattle. After a trip to California they returned to Nome. She worked again as a seamstress and house cleaner, but the money went quickly on medications for Bennett's tuberculosis. Ada married a second time. When her new husband found out that she had no money, he left her with another child. And then Ada, too, disappeared.

In 1935 a reporter spotted Ada walking on a remote beach in Alaska's Aleutian Islands. The only thing she said to him was that she needed to finish collecting firewood. In 1979 she visited Fred Maurer's nieces in Ohio. She was still as quiet and reserved as she had always been. Ada Blackjack died in 1983 at the age of eighty-five, a hero and a mystery to the end.

Dervla Murphy

1931–

Dervla Murphy received a bicycle and an atlas for her tenth birthday. It took her only a few days to decide that it would make perfect sense to ride that bicycle from her home in Ireland to India. After all, there was less ocean to cross on that route than on routes to other places, and she already had the urge to go far away. She would leave as soon as she could. "However, I was a cunning child so I kept my ambition to myself, thus avoiding the tolerant amusement it would have provoked among my elders ... I would cycle to India."

Not only was ten somewhat young to set off alone, but World War II was raging all over Europe. So Dervla began by taking her bicycle on longer and increasingly difficult rides in the country around her hometown of Lismore, in County Waterford, Ireland. At fourteen she had to leave school to care for her mother, who was ill, while her father continued to work as the county librarian. For the next sixteen years Dervla kept house and cared for her parents. She also read great literature, wrote adventure stories (all of which were rejected by publishers), and wrote to a Sikh girl in Kuala Lumpur. When she was past thirty, more than twenty years after her decision to travel, she was finally able to leave. And so on January 14, 1963, Dervla and "Roz," her thirty-seven-pound bike (named for Don Quixote's horse), set off for India—in the worst snowstorm on record.

It was a terrible beginning. All across Europe the winter turned out to be the worst in eighty years. She had expected an easy and pleasant ride through France and Italy. Instead, she rode through a nightmare of ice and snow. In Yugoslavia, Dervla stayed in a hostel for women who worked in a factory, and everyone had to be out of the hostel by five o'clock in the morning. The day she left there, she again thought she would have a pleasant ride. This time the wind made her miserable by blowing her right off her bicycle. As she climbed into the mountains, the wind diminished, but then the ice and snow began again. High in the mountains she got so cold and numb that she had to take refuge at a small inn; she stayed

Dervla riding her bicycle, "Roz," past some sheep in the German countryside, 1952.

there for two weeks before moving on.

> "I had always thought there was something faintly comical in the idea of being devoured by wolves. It seemed to me the sort of thing that doesn't really happen."
>
> —Dervla Murphy

Dervla rode in a truck from Zagreb to Belgrade. The road was so bad that the truck had to take a detour, and neither the driver nor Dervla knew where they were. In the dark, with all the ice and snow, the truck slid off the road into a tree. They had to get help. The driver was pinned in the truck, so Dervla started walking. A few minutes later, "a heavy weight hurled itself at me without warning," then another weight hit her leg. It was so dark that she couldn't tell what was attacking her, but they had eyes and teeth. She took out the pistol she had taken to protect herself, and shot the first wolf. The second wolf let go of her ankle and ran, and a third crept away. Finally, Dervla made it to the nearest town and got help.

From Yugoslavia she went to Bulgaria. Since the two countries were not friendly, the road had not been kept up, and travel was slow and difficult. When, Dervla wondered, would she be able to actually ride Roz, not just push her around?

In fact, Dervla was able to cycle through much of Bulgaria and Turkey and into Persia (now Iran). One night she woke to find all her bedding pulled off and a large man bending over her. She took her gun out from under her pillow, shot once at the ceiling, watched her intruder run away, and went back to sleep. Her friends, she remembered, had thought it silly to take a gun, but in the first few weeks of her trip she was twice glad she did. Still, she liked Persia and was sorry to leave it: "There is an elegance and dignity about life here which you can't appreciate at first."

In Teheran she was told she could not have a visa to go into Afghanistan, where two women had recently been killed in an anti–women's emancipation riot. Dervla also heard of two French women photographers who had been stoned and seriously injured. Finally, though, she got the visa, and on March 31, she rode her bicycle 175 kilometers (108 miles), arriving at the border of Afghanistan at six o'clock in the evening.

At last the weather was good, and the countryside she cycled through was breathtaking—quiet, bare hills, fields of wheat, and mud villages along the way. She quickly learned that the people did not like having their pictures taken. She passed areas where Afghanis lived in goatskin tents, she slept on the floor of a roadside teahouse, and since not being noticed was the safest way to travel, she tried to be as anonymous and discreet as she could.

Dervla was deeply impressed by the people of Afghanistan. She found them dignified and honorable. But the only women she met were in the burqa, a long garment which covered them so completely that she could not tell which way they were facing. "The only female face I've seen in the city [Herat] was that of a Mongolian tribeswoman down from the mountains, bringing cloth to sell in the bazaar; she was galloping along the main street, astride and bareheaded with a baby tied to her back." As long as Dervla did not take a camera, she was welcome to visit the mosques and stay as long as she wished, so she did.

Because she did not feel threatened in Afghanistan, she decided to leave Herat before dawn on the morning of April 13. Almost as soon as she got started, though, soldiers stopped her and told her she had to ride a bus to Kandahar. There seemed to be no real reason for this, but they had guns, so she took the bus. The only other two women were riding on top of the bus along with luggage and the goods that people were taking to market to sell. To make it worse, these women were very ill and were on their way to hospital in Kabul, a thousand-kilometer (625-mile) ride.

After two days in Kandahar, Dervla and Roz set out for Kabul, probably a five- or six-day journey. Heat, road conditions, and the conditions of mountain passes would influence that. So too, she realized, might bandits, who could grab her and Roz, and depending on her luck, drop them both in Kabul in two days—or never.

Dervla left Kandahar before daybreak. This time there were no soldiers and she covered 145 kilometers (90 miles) "across vast unpeopled widths of sand and barren sun-split clay ... at 3:30 p.m. furnace blasts of hot air were ricocheting off the face of the desert and even my hair was soaked with sweat." Nor was the sun the only source of discomfort: "I'm now aware all the time of a slight underlying tension which mars what would otherwise be a completely enjoyable experience ... Every Afghan I've met has said that he personally would not cycle alone through his own country."

She went to Kabul before cycling over the highest mountain yet, 3,200 meters (10,500 feet) above the Shibar Pass. From there she went to Bamiyan, formerly a major center of Buddhist religion. Outside the window where she stayed, a

On her way to India, Dervla cycled through glaciers (left) and over planks across deep crevasses (right) in the mountains of Afghanistan and Pakistan.

thirty-six-meter (120-foot) statue of Buddha stood in an alcove. Both the alcove and the statue were carved into the rock of the mountain. The caves nearby were full of statues, including one that was twenty-four meters (eighty feet) high. "Even though I was mentally prepared for those Buddhas the impact was tremendous when I actually saw them presiding impassively over the valley." In 2001, the Taliban smashed all of these Buddhas.

From there Dervla went on to explore the ruins of the "City of Sighs," where the King of Bamian defeated the great Mongol warrior Genghis Khan in 1222, almost 800 years ago. And then, on one of the few good roads she travelled, she made her way through the fabled Khyber Pass to Peshawar, in Pakistan. The contrast of fascinating and terrifying experiences continued. She loved the countryside. She met people from all walks of life. And in West Pakistan, the raja of the Punial Mountain State offered her a farm to live on for the rest of her life. (She turned him down, saying that she could not leave Ireland forever, but she did stay in his palace long enough to see all his massive gardens, which she compared to the Garden of Eden.) On the other hand, a riot broke out on a bus she rode on, and a rifle butt broke three of her ribs. And despite being an experienced, careful traveller, she

During the exhausting trip through the Tangi Sharo gorge in Afghanistan, Dervla fell asleep at the side of the road in the glaring midday sun. An elderly Afghan man built a tent over her so quietly that she didn't wake up!

suffered sunstroke, frostbite, and dysentery, any of which could have proved fatal. She was very aware of the ever-present and contrasting beauty, excitement, danger, and hardship of her journey.

She reached the border of India. The weather was too hot to try to ride Roz, so Dervla looked for something to do until she could continue her travels. The plight of the orphans she had seen along the way led her to volunteer to work with refugee children, most of them orphans from Tibet. She went to Dharamsala, at the edge of the Himalayas, home of the Dalai Lama, who had been exiled from Tibet. The children lived in shacks or with no shelter at all. They had little to eat or drink, and one nurse, one doctor, one cook, and several volunteers were trying to take care of more than a thousand children. Dervla worked there for six months.

Meanwhile, a story about her in an Indian newspaper created a flurry of interest in England. She was invited to send the story of her travels to John Murray Publishers, the same company that had published Freya Stark's books. Dervla never dreamed that her own book would be accepted, but it was. Now she, too, was on the way to writing many more accounts of her adventures.

Her next trip was to Abyssinia (now Ethiopia), in Africa, but this time she left Roz at home. The plan was to hike through the mountainous country. There was no such thing as a good map of this region, but Dervla figured that as long as she went due south from Massawah, she would eventually arrive at Addis Ababa, the capital.

Hiking with a heavy pack on her back and blisters on her feet was no fun. Friends introduced her to the eldest grandchild of the former Ethiopian Emperor Haile Selassie, Her Highness Leilt Aida Desta, who found a mule for her. Jock the mule and a donkey called Satan (for good reason—

he had a terrible temper) were a huge help, and in three months Dervla walked over 1,600 kilometers (1,000 miles).

Dervla stayed in Ireland after the birth of her daughter Rachel in 1968. Then, when Rachel was five, the two of them went to South India. The trip went so well that Dervla decided to journey on to Baltistan, also called Little Tibet. At that time Baltistan was part of the disputed territory between India and Pakistan. Her friends thought Dervla was crazy. She and Rachel walked and rode through five valleys, including the Indus Gorge, which is known for its bandits, flimsy bridges, and paralyzing snowfalls. They saw no other Westerners during the entire four months they were there, and they ate the local diet of apricots and hard-boiled eggs. The trip was such a success that they went back the next year.

Dervla and Rachel returned to Tibet and Nepal in 1975. On this trip Rachel got a terrible foot infection, which Dervla discovered after Rachel had walked for a long day without complaint or tears. Dervla operated on her daughter's foot in a village so that Rachel could make the rest of the trip to a doctor, who performed a second operation. At the end of it he told Dervla that she had done a wonderful job of cleaning up the infection, and that all he'd done was make sure it was gone. Clearly, the brave girl was growing up to be as intrepid as her mother.

In 1976 Dervla decided to cycle around her own country to explore the political and religious tensions that were tearing Ireland apart and causing so much death and destruction. The book she wrote about that trip shows how a person can be an explorer even in familiar territory.

> "Rachel is a natural stoic, and a muscular and vigorous little person, well able to walk ten or twelve miles a day without flagging."
>
> —Dervla Murphy

Next, Dervla and Rachel, now age nine, travelled with pack mules down the route the conquistadors had taken through Peru. They carried clothing for high altitudes, blankets, and a tent. The book Dervla would write about this journey looked into the history of the Incas and the Spanish who conquered them.

The nuclear accident at Three Mile Island in Pennsylvania took place in March 1979. Dervla, shocked by the destructive potential of such an accident, took time out to study and write about nuclear power, weapons, and the danger of producing nuclear energy. Then it was on to Madagascar. And Cameroon. To Transylvania, home of the Dracula legend. And South Africa.

Dervla's faithful bicycle Roz had long since retired. In 1992 Dervla gave herself a "Rolls-Royce of a mountain-bike," which she named Lear, and set off for a long, five-thousand-kilometer (three-thousand-mile) bicycle trip through Kenya, Uganda, Tanzania, Malawi, Zambia, and Zimbabwe. She started out thinking she would have a lovely time in the gorgeous terrain of Africa. And she did. She travelled by day and usually stayed in villages at night. She climbed mountains and glided down into valleys. But the trip turned out to be anything but carefree. She saw corruption and the results of massacres, countries whose economies were collapsing, "foreign aid plans" that accomplished nothing. And everywhere she saw evidence of the AIDS pandemic. Parents and children dying together. Villages of orphans. Children taking care of their parents and siblings. People dying on the side of the road. The book that came out of that African trip is called *The Ukimwi Road*. Ukimwi is the Swahili word for AIDS. This was a trip unlike any of the others.

A pandemic is an epidemic that ranges over a large geographical area. For example, between 25 and 50 million people died worldwide in the Spanish influenza (or "flu") pandemic of 1918 and 1919, including between five and seven hundred thousand in the U.S., and thirty thousand in Canada.

When she was just four years old, Dervla Murphy announced to her mother that she was going to write books. At ten, her dream of bicycling to India was born. The year she turned sixteen, she decided that she would stay independent all her life. Dervla is now over seventy, and she has done all those things and much, much more. She recently cycled through a remote part of Russia where there are no hotels, few roads, and almost no people. When she is not travelling, she lives where she was born, in Lismore, County Waterford, Ireland.

SHARON WOOD

1957–

SHARON WOOD STOOD AT THE TOP OF THE WORLD on May 26, 1986, the sixth woman—and the first North American woman—to reach the summit of Mount Everest, which soars 8,850 meters (nearly 30,000 feet) into the sky. As if that were not enough, the route she and her team had taken was a new one, and theirs was the first successful climb of that route without the help of Sherpas, the famed local Himalayan guides. It was getting dark and the temperature was dropping dangerously. After only twenty minutes at the top, Sharon and her teammate began the descent of the mountain. She had spent all her twenty-nine years preparing for those twenty minutes.

Sharon Wood was born in Halifax, Nova Scotia, on Canada's east coast, and grew up in Vancouver, British Columbia, on its west coast. She loved individual sports even as a very young child. When she was twelve she and her father climbed Sky Pilot Mountain on the coast of British Columbia. At sixteen she moved to Jasper, Alberta, the center of Canadian climbing. She worked as a guide at Maligne Lake and climbed every moment she could. In 1974, she participated in an Outward Bound program where she met Laurie Skreslet, the first Canadian to climb Mount Everest, who became her mentor and friend. Soon after the program, Sharon became a certified mountain guide and climbing instructor.

By the late 1970s, Sharon was climbing some of the world's highest mountains. In 1983 she reached the Cassin Ridge summit on Denali, also known as Mount McKinley, the highest peak in North America. The next year she was part of a five-person team of Canadians and Americans who spent three months on the West Ridge of Mount Makalu, 8,470 meters (nearly 28,000 feet) high in Nepal. A hundred meters (about 330 feet) from the top of the mountain, the weather prevented them from going the rest of the way. She also did major climbs in South America, notably Huascaran Sur at 6,769 meters (about 22,000 feet) high. On the second day of that five-day climb, falling rock hit Sharon—she continued the climb with a broken shoulder.

Many, perhaps all, serious mountain climbers dream of climbing Mount Everest. Few have the opportunity to try, and fewer make it. Being invited to be the only woman on the eleven-member Canadian Everest Light Expedition was a dream come true. The climb requires tremendous skill, strength, and experience. The weather is unpredictable at best and brutal at worst, and the peak of the mountain is so high that lack of oxygen is a serious problem for much of the climb. Any of these elements could defeat even the best climbers. This peak, almost four kilometers (two-and-a-half miles) straight up, has fascinated climbers and claimed their lives for centuries.

Sharon climbing Anquash face on Huascaran Sur, Peru.

The Canadian Everest Light Expedition planned to start from Tibet and climb the mountain's West Ridge, a particularly difficult route that is not often attempted. Timing is vital when going up Mount Everest. May is the best month as there is more light than most other months and less chance of vicious temperatures, blizzards, and howling winds. The possibility of avalanches, however, is always there. While Everest is never a friendly, easy place, it tends to be less hostile in May than at other times.

The expedition started at the established Base Camp from which all Everest expeditions begin. It is 5,182 meters (17,000 feet) above sea level and just over 3,500 meters (nearly 11,500 feet) directly below the peak. That distance would be an easy forty-five-minute stroll on flat terrain. On Everest, it would take the Light Team forty-five days.

Climbers go up large mountains in relays. Up and back to Base Camp. Further up, they set up a smaller camp, and go back to Base Camp. Smaller groups go further up and back to established camps, which the Base Camp supplies

"Climbers don't conquer mountains. The conquest occurs within the mind of the climber, in ... getting through to that good stuff – that stuff called potential, most of which we rarely use."

– Sharon Wood

with food and water. As the team goes higher, fewer people go on. Thus the team makes a chain up the mountain. This chain then supports the people who go to the very top.

The Everest Light team set up six camps on the side of the mountain. It was to the highest camp that Sharon and her climbing mate, Dwayne Congdon, had to return the night they reached the peak.

Despite supplies that are sent from Base Camp, each climber carries a tremendous load. Extra food and clothing, water, climbing gear, tents, sleeping bags, camp stoves, and supplies for fires and navigation: all these supplies go up any major mountain on the climbers' backs. Toward the top of Everest, each climber also carried fifteen kilograms (thirty-three pounds) of bottled oxygen.

The oxygen was essential. Without enough oxygen, blood flow slows down, muscles become weak, breathing becomes very difficult, and a person's brain stops functioning clearly, often leading to hallucinations. These dangers leave climbers vulnerable to faster freezing, especially of fingers and toes, to slow, awkward movements, and to poor judgment that can prove treacherous, or even fatal, for the most experienced climber.

The weather made for constant difficulties. The average temperature in the tents was minus 20°C (just below 0°F). It usually took more than two hours in the morning to melt enough snow for the daily supply of five to six liters (about ten pints) of water per climber per day. High winds meant that stoves had to be used inside the tents, and since that meant a small space with people, nylon, and open flames, cooking was truly dangerous. The right kind of clothing was essential, too. For example, custom-made suits of layers of material that breathed allowed climbers to sweat without having the sweat freeze against their bodies. And of course, the clothes had to allow easy movement and be warm without being bulky.

Because their lungs have adapted, the people of the high mountains in Tibet are able to breathe and function in places where others would die from oxygen deprivation.

All the climbers were experienced and had been chosen for their skill and stamina. Even still, as the expedition climbed, the strain increased, the weather got worse, and members of the expedition got sick. At Camp Five, half the team had to return to Base Camp. The wind was getting worse. As the wind increased, visibility decreased and the danger grew—to the point where there was some question whether the expedition would even try to make it to the top.

Sharon Wood, Barry Blanchard, Dwayne Congdon, and Kevin Doyle set out from Camp Five. They decided that Barry and Kevin would provide support while Sharon and Dwayne attempted to reach the summit. Sharon was chosen to make the final effort partly because she was a woman; if she made it, she would be the first North American woman to reach the summit of Mount Everest. A situation like this can be very uncomfortable for women: on the one hand, they want the opportunities they have earned and could be denied simply because they are women. On the other hand, they want these opportunities because they have earned them, not just because they are women. And a woman who is the first (that we know of) to do or attempt to do something feels an added responsibility to "make it," so that others will have more opportunity to be able to follow in her footsteps. Sharon felt all of this. They were so close. Part of her wanted to keep climbing, part of her wanted to stick to the original plan that Dwayne and Barry would go to the top, and part of her just wanted to go home. But if she didn't keep going, some other North American woman would be the first to reach the top. She had come this far. She decided to take the opportunity that her teammates were offering her.

As they climbed to what would be Camp Six, the winds increased to hurricane force, strong enough to blow a climber, even one with a heavy pack, off course, perhaps right off the mountain.

Barry and Kevin helped set up Camp Six and left for Base Camp. Sharon and Dwayne were now alone, just below the top of the world. This was a once-in-a-lifetime opportunity. Would they, could they, make it?

The summit, they thought, was less than ten meters (thirty-two feet) above them. They thought this final push would take only a few minutes. The wind howled. Snow blew everywhere. Breathing was difficult. An avalanche narrowly missed Sharon. That last few minutes' climb took over an hour.

At the top, Sharon and Dwayne hugged each other and took pictures. The wind ripped their Canadian flag out of Sharon's hands. Their oxygen was almost gone and they were exhausted. It was getting dark. They had stayed at the top of the world for a total of twenty minutes, but now they had to leave.

Going down a mountain can be more dangerous than going up, as Sharon knew well. Sharon went down the rope they had set up the day before. Since only one person can be on the ropes at a time, she then waited for Dwayne. And waited. There was no sign of him and now, she realized, the lack of oxygen was making her mind do strange things. She dozed off more than once. She lost track of time. How long had it been? Where was he? How long would it be until she froze right there at the bottom of that rope?

She had to keep going, to find the tent. In the dark, with

only a headlamp for light, Sharon was alone at the top of Mount Everest, with a brain that wanted to shut down from the cold and lack of oxygen, and a body that would quickly follow. Looking for the tent was like looking for a needle in a haystack. Finally, her light flashed off a used oxygen bottle. Six hours after leaving the summit, she had found the tent.

Everyone at Base Camp was awake and alert. Sharon and Dwayne had been out of radio contact for too long. It had turned dark while they were on the summit, and from below the watchers could see their headlamps. But the lamps were wandering farther and farther apart. Were the climbers in trouble?

It took Dwayne another hour and a half to get there. He had run out of oxygen just after leaving the top and that had given him trouble focusing and breathing. His fingers and toes had started to freeze and he had needed to stop several times to shake even a little feeling back into them.

In the tent, the exhausted pair needed water even more than they needed sleep. Sharon lit the stove to melt ice. What they didn't know was that it had a propane leak. The

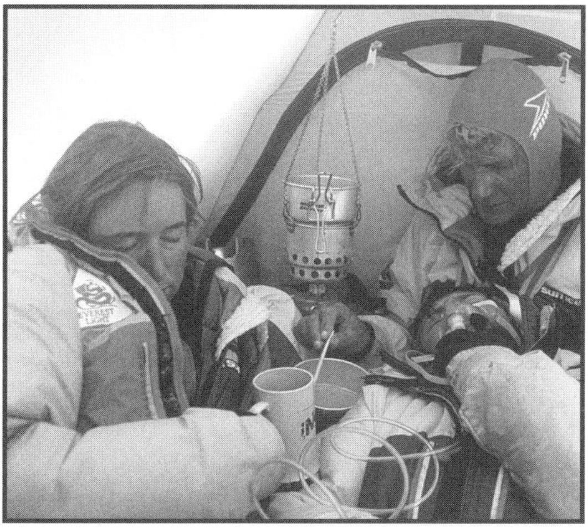

Sharon and Dwayne Congdon lie exhausted in a tent at Camp Five the day after reaching the summit of Everest in 1986. Sharon's friend and mentor, Laurie Skreslet, helps with their recovery.

stove exploded in front of her, shot out the door of the tent in flames and disappeared down the mountain. Water would have to wait.

The next morning Sharon and Dwayne set out down the mountain. The first Canadian expedition, the first North American woman, and the sixth woman ever had reached the summit of Everest, the mountain the people of Nepal call Sagarmatha, which can be translated as "Mother of the Universe" or "Goddess of the Sky."

What does a person do after she has done the impossible? Sharon's amazing achievement has brought her many awards. These include Professional Mountaineer of the Year, the Meritorious Service Award from the Governor-General of Canada, an honorary doctor of laws degree from the University of Calgary in Alberta, the Summit of Excellence Award at the Banff Mountain Film Festival, and the very first Tenzing Norgay Award, given by the American Alpine Club and the Explorers' Club of New York in the name of the Sherpa who made the first climb by Westerners of Mount Everest with Sir Edmund Hillary. Sharon Wood now has two sons and tours as a speaker, talking about the power of sharing a vision, and encouraging people to work together as a team to live their vision.

Sharon says her twenty years of professional climbing have taught her the following:
to turn a dream into reality;
to reach goals one step at a time;
and to work with a team to reach team and personal goals.

Matty McNair and Denise Martin

1952–

1966–

MATTY MCNAIR WENT ON HER FIRST CANOE TRIP when she was two weeks old. Later she worked for twenty-two years with the wilderness organization Outward Bound. Since 1984, she and her husband have run NorthWinds, an Arctic exploration company which, in November 2004, led its first expedition to the South Pole, in Antarctica. In 1996, when the twenty women of the Women's Polar Relay were looking for someone to lead an expedition from Ellesmere Island in Nunavut to the geographic North Pole, a distance of 416 nautical miles, Matty was their obvious choice.

Earlier that year, Caroline Hamilton, a British woman with a dream, had taken out a newspaper ad looking for nineteen other women to join her in a journey to the North Pole. Six hundred women replied to the ad, and from them the members of the Women's Polar Relay were chosen. They set out to raise $600,000 to pay for the expedition, and once the fundraising was under way, they contacted Matty.

Matty knew the dangers of the trip. Although several people have made the journey from Ellesmere Island to the North Pole over the last century, it is still a long, hard, and dangerous trek over ever-changing ice fields. The nine British teams who tried it before the Women's Polar Relay had all failed. Matty made it clear that she would only lead an expedition that was fully ready and had the best and most appropriate equipment available.

The negotiations were long and difficult. The organizers wanted a man to be co-leader. Matty said no: if this was to be a women's expedition, it would be a women's expedition—no men. Her choice for a co-leader was Denise Martin. She and Denise had worked together before, and Matty knew that Denise's skills complemented hers. Denise had started her outdoor training at seventeen with Katimavik, then for nearly a decade had been an instructor with Outward Bound. She was eager to co-lead the expedition.

Next, Matty wanted complete decision-making authority in the choice of equipment and supplies. Her biggest rule is: *In the Arctic, if you get wet, you die.* She would choose everything: flashlights, camp stoves, clothing, skis, boots, socks, and enough of the right kind of food for twenty-two women who needed to consume between 4,500 and 5,000 calories a

Members of the expedition included a journalist, a chiropractor, a physiotherapist, a film producer, and a full-time mom. The women ranged from twenty-one to fifty-one years of age, and two of them were mother and daughter.

day for up to seventy days. Eventually it was agreed that Matty would lead the expedition in the way she knew would be most safe and likely to succeed. Even at that, she figured the group had a fifty-fifty chance of reaching their goal. Nothing was certain. There was no possible way to assure safety, but the odds were good enough.

Eight days before departure, much of the clothing still had not arrived. When it finally did turn up, Matty discovered that the proposed co-leader she had rejected in favor of Denise Martin had replaced the one-piece suits she had ordered with suits that, in the Arctic, would kill the people wearing them. Because these suits did not breathe, they would collect sweat, which would then cool, making the temperature of the women wearing them drop. Eventually the water in the suit would freeze, and the wearer would die. The same thing happened with the boots and socks. The skis Matty had specified had also been replaced. The skis they got were not strong enough and were too short to be able to cross a gap in the ice. Matty secured one in a vise and then bent it with one hand until it broke. Frustrating and expensive last-minute replacements of some equipment and changes to the suits and socks almost delayed the start of the expedition.

Finally, on the afternoon of March 14, 1997, the group flew in to Ellesmere Island and started out. Matty wrote in her journal: "I feel at home. I am in my element: ice, snow, cold, and limitless horizons. My heart swells to embrace the magic."

The twenty British women worked in five teams of four. The plan was that each team would be on the ice for fourteen to seventeen days, covering about eighty-three nautical miles and keeping as close to schedule as possible so

A nautical mile is 1.14 statute miles or 1.85 kilometers, so 416 nautical miles is the equivalent of about 474 statute miles or 770 kilometers.

The expedition is underway!

they would not run out of food. When it was time to change teams, the team that was out on the ice would find a place where a small plane could land, and then radio their position. A plane would pick up the team that was finished and drop off the next relay team and more supplies. Matty and Denise would be the only two to make the entire journey.

It's easy (and dangerous) to underestimate the North. Its great white expanses look solid. But polar ice, which has been three-and-a-half meters (eleven-and-a-half feet) thick for most of the time people have been measuring it, is now in most places no more than two-and-a-half meters (over eight feet). This is probably part of the process of global warming. Whatever the reason, because the ice is now thinner than it has ever been, it is more difficult and treacherous to cross. Without experienced, strong, and sensible leadership, this expedition, like so many others, could easily have failed—or worse.

Alpha Team set out. Each woman was pulling a heavily loaded pulk (a cross between a boat and a sled, made of very light material). One of their first discoveries was that the salami Matty had ordered, which was to be the main source of fat for the high-fat diet the women needed for energy and strength, had been substituted with cheaper meat. The meat was so bad that no one could eat it, and they wound up throwing away three kilograms (nearly seven pounds) of precious food.

In their first few days, Alpha Team had to climb huge

pressure ridges, with ice blocks the size of buildings. In some places the ice was soft. In others it was cracked or cracking, so that it was never possible to know exactly what they were skiing on or whether it would support a person and a loaded pulk.

By the tenth day, visibility was two meters (six-and-a-half feet) in high winds and blowing snow. On Day 11 they realized that the ice was drifting eastward, toward Greenland and away from the North Pole. On Day 12, after staying in their tent for two days, the women set out onto a maze of cracks, loose ice, and moving rubble. When their radio broke down, the surgeon and chiropractor in the group performed an operation on the battery to get it to work.

Team Bravo landed on Day 17. Matty was dangerously cold, couldn't use her fingers, and recognized that her judgment was impaired. With 360 of the 416 nautical miles to go, all she wanted was to go home. Instead, she greeted Team Bravo and prepared to go on with the second team of the relay.

As they skied, the ice started to resemble huge heads of cauliflower, as well as the usual blocks of ice and chunks of rubble. One of the women was getting perilously cold. Then, the bindings on the skis started to break, one after another. Without healthy team members and reliable equipment, the expedition would not be able to continue. But Matty managed to improvise a way to repair the bindings, and the team pushed on. On Day 27 the team members were particularly glad to have repaired bindings: they had to cross a six-meter (twenty-foot) drop in which only the length of a ski kept each woman from certain death in the icy water. The skis got both the women and all the equipment across.

Day 28 was planned to be the next

> "The major difference between our expedition and the men's expeditions is that we took care of ourselves."
>
> — Matty McNair

switchover. It had been difficult to find a good airstrip because the ice was too soft, but Matty, Denise, and Team Bravo were ready. The plane didn't arrive. Nor did it show up the next day. Finally, on Day 30, in poor visibility in the middle of the night, the plane arrived with Team Charlie, food, batteries, and new bindings for the skis.

During Team Charlie's first day out, Denise jumped a crack in the ice. The snow on the far side gave way and she fell into the water. Matty's motto went through her head: *In the Arctic, if get wet you die.* Fortunately, Denise's waterproof clothing worked, and she scrambled out without getting soaked.

The next few days with the new team went very well, and the group covered almost nine nautical miles a day. But Team Charlie's fifth day, several of the team members had bad coughs. They had overextended themselves. Then the weather cooperated with them—it got so bad that they had to take a much-needed day off. The wind was gusting to eighty kilometers (fifty miles) an hour, the visibility was 100 meters (328 feet), and the temperature was minus 23°C (about minus 5°F). The expedition members slept almost until noon, repaired tears in their equipment and the tent, and didn't even try to go anywhere.

The ice kept drifting east, carrying the expedition farther and farther away from the Pole. But the team needed to keep going, and the next day they set out despite a strong wind. Then one of the women, Sue, sank into the ice. She climbed out, but almost immediately sank again with two others. The water grabbed Denise. Sue lost a boot and was in the frigid water in just her socks. One of the pulks fell into the water, and it was so heavily packed that they couldn't get it back up. Their one and only tent wound up floating in open water.

Meanwhile, an opening fifty meters (over 160 feet) wide

"The ice is incredible. I found it so fascinating and beautiful. The world underfoot was ever changing. Life on the ice becomes simple and deeply satisfying and revolves around the three themes of food, shelter, and companionship."

— Denise Martin

appeared in the ice, stretching as far north and south as anyone could see. Three of the women were on the east side of it, three on the west. Denise swam in the frigid water to retrieve the tent and radio. Finding Sue's boot was harder, but Denise managed it. When she had rescued as much of the equipment as she could out of the water, the stoves were on one side of the open water and the tent and radio on the other. If they could not get across the opening, half the expedition would have to spend the night with stoves but no tent, the other half with a tent but no stoves. Either way could prove fatal. There was no way to cross such a wide opening, but the women had to get together and get dry.

Then, as can happen in the Arctic, the ice shifted again and the opening closed as quickly as it had appeared. With a crashing roar, the connecting ice, which had been dangerous mush, became hard as cement. Thanks to Denise's strength and skill, the group only lost a total of six ski poles.

The team named this area the "hell zone." The next day the ice bridge that had saved them was gone. So was their confidence. As they went on, they found themselves crossing ice that minutes later would disappear. While they were crossing a high ridge, it started to move and shake. One woman lost her balance, and her ski pole ripped a hole in the shoulder of the one-piece suit of the woman in front of her, exposing her to the cold and wind. There was no choice but to keep going until they found solid ice to camp on. When they finally set up the tent and started the stoves, they climbed in, feeling warm and cozy—and safe—even though they knew that anything could happen. The ice was secure for the moment, but it was still drifting. They had set out for the North Pole. Would they wind up in Greenland instead?

Team Charlie was due to go home on Day 43, but the ice was covered with huge chunks of ice rubble. No plane could land. Over the next couple of days, one of the women started to get sick. Visibility was poor. The members of Team Charlie talked of hot showers, washing their hair, and good food. This was a hard time for Matty and Denise. They had not had different food, a shower, or clean hair in forty-two days, and they had at least another four weeks on the ice.

At three o'clock on the morning of Day 46, they found a strip where a plane could land. In sixteen days, skiing nine nautical miles a day, they had moved only seventy-one nautical miles north. Team Charlie had finished their work. Knowing that she, Denise, and the next two relay teams had to keep going, Matty began to wonder if she would burn out on this trip.

Team Delta arrived with energetic women, supplies, letters from home, and chocolate. On their second day out, they reached the halfway mark. Conditions improved, and the eastward drift stopped. They had to hurry to beat the spring thaw, but life had definitely improved. In her journal Matty wrote, "The wings of my spirit could extend to the far horizons." Then she added, "I've been eating the same food for 49 days!"

Matty had wondered if the ice that had drifted so far east might turn and shift west, pushing them closer to the Pole. On May 1 that westward drift started. Now they were really moving!

> "We didn't conquer the Arctic; we came to move across it and learn from it."
>
> – Matty McNair

It would not all be smooth going, though. Rough terrain and lots of ice rubble slowed them down to the point where they skied a disappointing eight kilometers (five miles) in eight-and-a-half hours. Diesel fuel got into their breakfast cereal, and they had to throw it away. And Matty was too cold; something was wrong. "I wonder if it is the ice in the air or if I have lost so much body fat that I am more vulnerable to the cold," she wrote. Her feet were sore and painful. Her back hurt. She was exhausted. If she got sick that would be the end of the expedition.

The westward drifting continued. On Day 54 there were 159 nautical miles to go. The next day, May 7, was Matty's wedding anniversary. She missed her family. She missed travelling with sled dogs. She missed home.

The team saw a seal and large polar bear tracks. They sat out a snowy day in the tent, trying not to become too concerned about the increasing cracks in the ice and the black water the cracks revealed.

Once again, bad weather delayed the plane bringing the next—and final—team. The weather cleared but the plane still didn't come. Finally, it showed up. Matty just about got on it, but again she decided to stick it out.

Team Echo arrived on Day 65. There were 110 nautical miles to go. Getting this close, tensions started to build. There was talk among the organizers of removing Matty and Denise as leaders so that Pen Hadow, the originally proposed co-leader who had made all the substitutions of supplies, could lead the group to the North Pole.

Matty and Denise, co-leaders of the expedition, at the North Pole.

Matty was furious. So were most of the expedition members. How dare the organizers even think about pulling in a man to lead a women's expedition in its very last moments of thrill and fame? The tension almost defeated Matty, almost did what the weather, the eastward drift, the danger, and the cold and wet couldn't do. But she was the leader of this expedition, she had come this far, and she was not going to let anyone take the final moments away from her. Pen stayed where he was.

On Day 74, her thirty-first birthday, Denise Martin became the first Canadian woman to reach the North Pole. It had been a harrowing adventure, filled with danger, surprise, and desperately hard physical challenges. But Matty and Denise had kept going through it all, the only members of the relay team to complete the entire journey, 416 treacherous nautical miles from Ellesmere Island to the North Pole.

Resources

Places to look for more women explorers:

Leon, Vicki. *Uppity Women of the New World.* Boston: Conari, 2001.

Miller, Luree. *On Top of the World: Five Women Explorers in Tibet.* London: Paddington Press, 1976.

Robinson, Jane. *Unsuitable for Ladies.* London: Oxford, 2001.

Stanley, Jo, ed. *Bold in Her Breeches: Women Pirates across the Ages.* New York: HarperCollins, 1995.

Stefoff, Rebecca. *Women of the World: Women Travelers and Explorers.* New York: Oxford, 1992.

Tinling, Marion. *Women into the Unknown: A Sourcebook on Women Explorers and Travelers.* New York: Greenwood, 1989.

CoolWomen: www.coolwomen.ca

Wikipedia, the Free Encyclopedia: http://en.wikipedia.org

Try Google or your library for these women: Gertrude Bell, Isabella Lucy Bird Bishop, Lady Anne Blunt, Bessie Coleman, Isak Dinesen, Amelia Earhart, Matty Gunterman, Mary Kingsley, Ella Maillart, Beryl Markham, Martha Martin, Lady Mary Wortley Montagu, Florence Nightingale, Annie Smith Peck, Ida Reye Pfeiffer, Martha Root, Mary Sheldon, Lady Hester Stanhope, May Kellogg Sullivan, Mary Schaffer Warren

Sacagawea

Blassingame, Wyatt. *Sacagawea: Indian Guide.* Champaign, IL: Garrard Publishing, 1965.

Clark, Ella E., and Margot Edmonds. *Sacagawea of the Lewis and Clark Expedition.* Berkeley: University of California Press, 1979.

Frazier, Neta Lohnes. *Sacagawea: The Girl Nobody Knows.* New York: David McKay, 1967.

Hunsaker, Joyce Badgley. *Sacagawea Speaks: Beyond the Shining Mountains with Lewis & Clark.* Guilford, CT: TwoDot, 2001.

St. George, Judith. *Sacagawea.* New York: Putnam, 1997.

Amanda Berry Smith

Bracey, John H., Jr. "Amanda Berry Smith." In *Notable American Women,* vol. 3, ed. Edward T. James and others. Cambridge: Harvard University Press, 1971.

Israel, Adrienne. "Amanda Berry Smith." In *Black Women in America: An Historical Encyclopedia,* vol. 2, ed. Darlene Clark Hine and others. Brooklyn, NY: Carlson, 1993.

Smith, Amanda Berry. *An Autobiography.* New York: Oxford, 1988 [1893]. Reissued as part of the Schomberg Library of Nineteenth Century Black Women Writers. Also available online at: http://docsouth.unc.edu/smitham/smith.html

Chicken Bones: A Journal for Literary and Artistic African-American Themes: www.nathanielturner.com/amandasmith.htm

Columbia County: http://muweb.millersville.edu/~ugrr/tellingstories/demosite/Columbia

Illinois Periodicals Online Project: www.lib.niu.edu/ipo/ihwt9820.html

Edith Watson and Victoria Hayward

Canadian Magazine of Politics, Science, Literature, and Art. Issues 1910-1926.

Hayward, Victoria, and Edith S. Watson. *Romantic Canada.* Toronto: Macmillan, 1922.

Rooney, Frances. *Working Light: The Wandering Life of Photographer Edith S. Watson.* Montreal and United Kingdom: McGill-Queen's University Press and Images Publishing, 1996.

__. "Edith S. Watson: Rural Canadians at Work, 1890-1920." Exhibition Catalogue. Sackville, New Brunswick: Owens Art Gallery, Mount Allison University, 1991.

__. "Finding Edith S. Watson." *Resources for Feminist Research.* Vol. 12 no. 1, 1983.

__. "Edith S. Watson, Photographer, and Victoria Hayward, Writer." *Fireweed* 13, 1982.

Alexandra David-Néel

David-Néel, Alexandra. *The Secret Oral Teachings of Tibetan Buddhist Sects.* Trans. from the French. San Francisco: City Lights, 1967.

David-Néel, Alexandra. *My Journey to Lhasa: The Personal Story of the Only White Woman Who Succeeded in Entering the Forbidden City.* New York: Harper, 1927.

__. *Tibetan Journey.* London: John Lane, 1936.

Miller, Luree. *On Top of the World: Five Women Explorers in Tibet.* London: Paddington Press, 1976.

Alexandra David-Néel Foundation and Cultural Centre, Digne-les-Bains, France: www.alexandra-david-neel.org

Phyllis Munday

Bridge, Kathryn. *Phyllis Munday, Mountaineer.* Montreal: Quest, 2002.

Smith, Cyndi. *Off the Beaten Track.* Lake Louise, AB: Coyote Books, 1989.

Whyte Museum of the Canadian Rockies: www.whyte.org

Canada Post: Phyllis Munday stamp: www.canadapost.ca/personal/collecting

Famous Canadian Women: http://famouscanadianwomen.com

Freya Stark

Geniesse, Jane Fletcher. *Passionate Nomad: The Life of Freya Stark.* New York: Random, 1999.

Izzard, Molly. *Freya Stark: A Biography.* London: Hodder & Stoughton, 1993.

Moorehead, Caroline. *Freya Stark.* New York: Penguin, 1985.

Robinson, Jane. *Unsuitable for Ladies.* London: Oxford, 2001.

Stefoff, Rebecca. *Women of the World: Women Travelers and Explorers.* New York: Oxford, 1992.

Tinling, Marion. Women into the Unknown: A Sourcebook on Women Explorers and Travelers. New York: Greenwood, 1989.

About Freya Stark: www.kypros.org/PIO/cyprus_today/jan_jun98/in_the_footsteps_of_freya_stark.htm

Ada Blackjack

Niven, Jennifer. *Ada Blackjack: A True Story of Survival in the Arctic.* New York: Hyperion, 2003.

Petrone, Penny. *Northern Voices: Inuit Writing in English.* Toronto: University of Toronto Press, 1988.

Stefansson, Vilhjalmur. *The Adventure of Wrangel Island.* New York: Macmillan, 1925.

McClanahan, Alexandra J. "Heroine of Wrangel Island." Lit Site Alaska (University of Alaska, Anchorage): http://lit sitealaska.edu.uss/aktraditions/wrangell.html (*Note: in the website address, Wrangel is spelled with an extra l — wrangell. This may refer to the town of Wrangell on main land Alaska, not Wrangel Island*)

Williams, Laura. "Wild Russia: A Look at Wrangel Island." Center for Russian Nature Conservation: http://wild-russia.org/bioregion1/1-wrangel/1_wrangel.htm

Dervla Murphy

Murphy, Dervla. *The Ukimwi Road: From Kenya to Zimbabwe.* London: John Murray, 1993.

__. *Wheels within Wheels: Autobiography.* London: John Murray, 1979.

__. *Where the Indus Is Young: A Winter in Baltistan.* London: John Murray, 1977.

__. *Full Tilt: From Ireland to India with a Bicycle.* London: John Murray, 1965.

Tinling, Marion. *Women into the Unknown: A Sourcebook on Women Explorers and Travelers.* New York: Greenwood, 1989.

Best of Bicycling: www.ahands.org/cycling/bicycling/dervla.html

Irish Writers Online: www.irishwriters-online.com

Wikipedia, the Free Encyclopedia: http://en.wikipedia.org/wiki/Dervla_Murphy

Sharon Wood

Rolfe, Helen Y. *Women Explorers: One Hundred Years of Courage and Audacity.* Canmore, AB: Altitude, 2003.

Wood, Sharon. Telephone conversation with the author, February 12, 2005.

Banff Centre: www.banffcentre.ca

Sharon Wood: www.sharonwood.net

Speakers Bureau: www.nsb.com.speaksbio

Matty McNair and Denise Martin

McNair, Matty. *On Thin Ice: A Woman's Journey to the North Pole.* Iqaluit, NU: NorthWinds, 1999.

Portraits. A Day Book. Charlottetown, PEI: gynergy, 1998.

Saskatoon Women's Calendar Collective. *Herstory 1999: The Canadian Women's Calendar.* Saskatoon : Saskatoon Women's Calendar Collective, 1998.

CoolWomen: www.coolwomen.ca

Iqaluit community website: www.denedeh.com

NorthWinds: www.northwinds-arctic.com

Photo Credits

Front cover

Sharon Wood: photo by Carlos Buhler

Matty McNair and Denise Martin: Matty McNair/Northwinds

Sacagawea:State Historical Society of North Dakota 0274-02

Ada Blackjack: Dartmouth College Library

Edith Watson (background): photo courtesy of Frances Rooney

Phyllis Munday: British Columbia Archives H-03440

Map (background): Dervla Murphy

Sacagawea

Pages 11 and 17: State Historical Society of North Dakota 0274-02

Page 13: Denver Public Library, Western History Collection, X-32254

Page 19: Denver Public Library, Western History Collection, Sawyers, X-32261

Amanda Berry Smith

Photos courtesy of Documenting the American South (http://docsouth.unc.edu), The University of North Carolina at Chapel Hill Libraries, North Carolina Collection

Edith Watson and Victoria Hayward

All photos courtesy of Frances Rooney

Alexandra David-Néel

Photos courtesy of Fondation Alexandra David-Néel, Digne-les-Bains, France

Phyllis Munday

Page 51: British Columbia Archives H-03440

Page 55: British Columbia Archives I-61980

Page 57: British Columbia Archives I-61976

Freya Stark

Page 61: Middle East Centre Archive, St. Antony's College, Oxford. Freya Stark Collection Ref 90 D3

Page 65: Middle East Centre Archive, St. Antony's College, Oxford. Freya Stark Collection Ref 32 D2

Page 68: Middle East Centre Archive, St. Antony's College, Oxford. Freya Stark Collection Ref 90 E1

Ada Blackjack

Photos courtesy of Dartmouth College Library

Dervla Murphy

Page 81: photo by Hallam Murray

Page 82: photo by Dervla Murphy

Page 85: photos by Dervla Murphy

Page 86: photo by Ruth Weller

Sharon Wood

Page 91: photo by Tod Korol, 2003

Page 93: photo by Carlos Buhler

Page 97: photo by Dan Griffiths

Matty McNair and Denise Martin

Page 99: Matty McNair photo courtesy of Matty McNair/NorthWinds
Denise Martin photo courtesy of University of Saskatchewan Archives (donated by the Saskatchewan Women's Calendar Collective)

Page 102: Matty McNair/NorthWinds

Page 107: Matty McNair/NorthWinds

THE 7 DAY STARTUP

THE 7 DAY STARTUP

YOU DON'T LEARN UNTIL YOU LAUNCH

DAN NORRIS

FOREWORD BY ROB WALLING

The 7 Day Startup

ISBN 13: 978-1502472397

10 9 8 7 6 5 4 3 2 1

CONTENTS

FOREWORD

by Rob Walling

I first heard about Dan Norris when he emailed to pitch me on a guest post called 13 Pre-Launch Traffic Strategies for Startups[1].

No wait… that's not right.

The first time I *actually* heard about Dan Norris was on the Tropical MBA[2] podcast—the hosts mentioned Dan's (now defunct) startup Inform.ly.

---

1 Dan Norris, "Case Study: 13 Pre-Launch Traffic Strategies for Startups (Part 3 of 3)," *Software by Rob*, accessed August 23, 2014, http://www.softwarebyrob.com/2012/11/06/case-study-13-pre-launch-traffic-strategies-for-startups-part-3-of-3/.

2 "Location Independent Entrepreneurship," *TMBA*, accessed August 23, 2014, http://www.tropicalmba.com/.

Umm… that's not right, either.

It was when Dan launched his podcast…

His blog…

His email newsletter…

Or when he put himself in the hotseat on Jason Calcanis' This Week in Startups[3].

I think you're starting to get the picture… The scary truth is that *Dan Norris is a hustler.*

In fact, there are few who can match Dan's *sheer volume of hustle*, be it when cranking out podcast episodes, blog posts, or putting himself out there on other peoples' podcasts (mine included[4]). I've always admired this about him.

---

3 Jason Calcanis, "Episode: 297: All Ask Jason - TWiST #297," *TWiST* video, 1:12:29, October 16, 2012, http://thisweekinstartups.com/all-ask-jason-twist-297/.

4 "Episode 183 | 5 Startup Rules to Live By with Dan Norris," *Startups For the Rest of Us*, accessed August 23, 2014, http://www.startupsfortherestofus.com/episodes/episode-183-5-startup-rules-to-live-by-with-dan-norris.

It's this hustle that enabled him to iterate, pivot, and brute force his way through multiple failed startup attempts and arrive at a standout success, WP Curve. And he went from spending six months to find his first paying customer to spending 7 Days.

I've worked with thousands of entrepreneurs over the years through my podcast[5], blog[6], startup conference[7], and my most recent startup[8]. Without question, the biggest mistake people make is obsessing over their idea and not focusing enough on finding people willing to pay for their product.

The 7 Day Startup is based on the hard knocks Dan has endured while launching idea after idea. He architected this book to get you from zero to paying customer in 7 Days and

5 "Startups For the Rest of Us," *Startups For the Rest of Us*, accessed August 23, 2014, http://www.startupsfortherestofus.com/.

6 Rob Walling, "Lessons Learned by a Solo Entrepreneur," *Software by Rob*, accessed August 23, 2014, http://www.softwarebyrob.com/.

7 "MicroConf - The Conference for Self-Funded Startups and Single Founders," *Micropreneur Academy, LLC*, accessed August 23, 2014, http://www.microconf.com/.

8 "Drip: Email Marketing Automation for Visitors, Trials and Customers," *Drip*, accessed August 23, 2014, https://www.getdrip.com/.

he's distilled his lessons into relatable stories and actionable takeaways to get you started as quickly as possible.

I know what you're thinking: "7 Days?! Has all this hustle rotted his brain? No one can launch an idea in 7 days."

And to that I offer a story:

When I interviewed Dan I, too, was incredulous at the thought of getting an idea out the door in 7 days. My email marketing startup, Drip[9], was as minimally viable as you can imagine, and it *still* took months to launch.

Dan's response to my pushback?

"I think it's worth considering whether or not Drip is a good idea for a first time entrepreneur who's bootstrapping. [In my book I have a] list of criteria for good ideas and one of them is the ability to build and test quickly.

Drip might be a good idea for a 3rd or 4th time entrepreneur, but it may not be a good idea for a first time entrepreneur

9 "Drip: Email Marketing Automation for Visitors, Trials and Customers," *Drip*, https://www.getdrip.com/.

because it might be too hard and too competitive to build something like that."

Well said, sir.

If you're a third- or fourth-time entrepreneur, I would hope you have it dialed in by now. Everyone else: you'd be well advised to listen to him.

I wish you all the best on your journey,

Rob Walling
Fresno, CA
August, 2014

YOU DON'T LEARN UNTIL YOU LAUNCH

"It's fine to celebrate success but it is more important to heed the lessons of failure." **Bill Gates**

In 2007, I was one year into my first business. Flying back from my honeymoon, I finished the book *Think and Grow Rich*. It advised thinking of a financial goal for the next 12 months, and saying it every day. I thought of $100k as an annual wage, to pay myself from my business profits. The maximum I could draw at the time was $40k, which was about half of what I was earning at my previous job a year earlier.

I said it to myself every day throughout 2007.

But I didn't hit the goal. I didn't even hit half of the goal. Not in 2007, or 2008, or 2009, or 2010, or 2011. In 2012, my wage dropped so far it fell below zero.

In June 2013, I had nothing left and was two weeks away from giving up on entrepreneurship for good and getting a job.

Flicking through the limited opportunities in my area, I considered moving my family back to the city. I'd thought of myself as an entrepreneur for the last fourteen years, and I'd ridden the roller coaster of business ownership for the last seven.

What the hell was the point?

My First Business Idea

In the year 2000 I was a long-haired twenty-year-old, struggling through a business degree at university. Bored out of my brain, I needed to choose an elective to make up for the courses I had failed, and stumbled across a brand new subject called "Entrepreneurship."

I dreamed of launching and running my own successful startup.

The objective was to come up with a business idea and plan how to make it happen. I figured it made sense to choose at least one course that taught me about starting and running a business, since that is what I was studying.

At that time you used Dogpile or Hotbot to search the web. There wasn't much there; all the good stuff was in the library. One day I came across a publication called the Ultimate HR Manual. As a Human Resources major, I hid it behind a stack of musty books in the never-used frog anatomy section. It couldn't leave the building—it was too powerful.

The manual held all the secrets for managing human resources. It outlined exactly how to hire and fire, how to recruit amazing talent, how to manage change, how to build a team, and how to train. It was the holy grail of HR.

I needed a business idea for my course, and after I discovered the HR manual, it dawned on me:

What if I put the HR manual... online?

I could create a site where business owners could access all the forms and processes required for best practicing HR, including position descriptions, employee surveys, HR Audits, and training programs. That would be cool! Wouldn't it?

My first business idea was born.

Over the next six months I mapped out the idea and planned exactly what topics to include, how to deliver the documents, how to charge, and even how to employ writers.

This was going to make me my first million. HR managers were already paying thousands for HR staff, so I figured they would certainly pay a few hundred dollars for every document they could ever need. As far as my research revealed, nothing like this existed.

I was proud of my plan—it was organized, meticulous, and thorough. Nervously submitting the assignment with hopes of earning a great mark, I waited… and *waited* for the results. Finally, the day came. I opened the assignment and saw an A. BOOM!

There was one problem: I didn't launch the business.

Sure, I had created a beautiful business plan after spending countless hours in the library deep diving into painstaking research.

But launching a business wasn't in the marking criteria.

Looking back, the timing was perfect. I had this idea just after the first dot com crash, and services like this became mainstream a few years later. HR documents and policies were easy to share and buy online. In hindsight, I'm sure it had the potential to be a seven- or eight-figure business.

I will never know for sure. You can never predict what happens after you start a business. Long-term plans and detailed documents are pointless. Most businesses go on to do something very different from what they set out to do. Today, this is called a pivot.

I learned a very valuable lesson from my failure to launch.

That lesson is: "You don't learn until you launch."

My First Business

The term "business" can mean different things to different people. If you buy a lawn mowing franchise, you are technically in business. But you are really just working for yourself.

The entrepreneur is the person who sold you the franchise. They created something from scratch, in extreme uncertainty with a high potential reward.

In 2006 I had just earned a promotion at my cushy corporate role, was 26, and finally ready to start a business. I told my co-workers that I would be a millionaire before I was 30.

My newest business idea was building websites for people. The fact that I didn't know how to build a website and had no IT qualifications didn't bother me. Instead, I threw myself in the deep end, learning rapidly from reading books and doing the work. My new clients would ask me questions like, "Can you build a website using ASP?"

I would say yes, then frantically search Google to find out what ASP was and get to work.

Everything looked great early on. I landed a project in my first week and earned $40,000 in my first year. Sure, it wasn't exactly $1,000,000—but I was happy to have even lasted a whole year!

In year two, I generated around $80,000 in revenue and by year three I had eclipsed the hallowed six-figure mark.

Before I knew it I had an office, local employees, a server, a phone system, hundreds of clients, and an influx of new leads. I had built a real business. I was on the path to becoming a millionaire. Or so I thought.

I had one major problem:

The business was not profitable.

It wasn't profitable in year one, year seven, or anywhere in between. I didn't become a millionaire before 30. I went backwards as all of my friends went forward. I was 30, living week to week, renting and earning a lower wage than anyone I knew.

It got worse before it got better.

I realized that bringing in more revenue wouldn't solve my profitability problem. The business was not growing. I tried everything, and I mean *everything*, to make it work. No matter what I did, I couldn't move the needle.

I'd have big successes like winning a $20,000 project, and then a big failure like writing off a $10,000 invoice or hiring the wrong person. It was never consistent.

I even bought another company for $40,000, thinking I'd add straight "profit to the bottom line." My revenue went up by $40,000 and so did my costs.

I regularly worked at Christmas time to appease my worst clients. I struggled with loneliness, a lack of motivation, and confidence. I had put myself out there, leaving my friends and co-workers. I knew people expected big things. *I* expected big things. I had never expected to fail.

There were plenty of positive signs where I'd think things were going to work out, but then something would change and I'd be knocked back on my arse again. This. Happened. All. The. Time.

I lost faith in my own judgment and committed to various courses of action, thinking they would save my business, only to have each one fail. After seven years in business I was turning over about $180,000 per year, but was still only making around $40,000 per year. I had never got even close to my honeymoon goal of a $100,000 salary.

In the end, I accepted that it was a problem I couldn't solve. I sold the business to build something new.

This time, I was going all in. I wanted to build something real. A startup that would succeed spectacularly. I wanted to stop scraping by and finally become a success. I wasn't leaving any room for the alternative.

My First Startup

There was enough money from the sale of my first business to cover 12 months of expenses. If I couldn't get traction by then, I would have to move cities and get a job. This was scary, but it didn't seem like a real threat because I was confident that I could make it work.

I knew what to do this time. I was going to create something big, something that could scale. I had four possible ideas I could run with.

1. A pot plant stand that supported heavy pots—a friend had told me they couldn't find one.
2. A surfing app that allowed surfers to check into their local break—think Foursquare for surfers.
3. An SEO app that enabled website owners to order SEO services for keywords.
4. An analytics dashboard that simplified analytics from various places.

I had no idea about product design or manufacturing, so the pot plant stand was out. I couldn't foresee making any money from the surfing app, so that was out too. I started building the SEO app and Google introduced new rules that punished that style of link building. Strike Three.

The analytics dashboard was the remaining idea, so I ran with it. I called it Web Control Room at first and later renamed it *Informly* to make it sound more like a startup.

Throughout the twelve months, most of the time I felt things were going well; there was good traction on the website, a lot of free signups, and regular press coverage. I had a great team and we put together a solid application that was unique, useful, and solved a big problem. Or so some people said.

After eleven months of trying everything, I was earning just $476 in recurring monthly revenue and spending $2,000+ a month. I had burned through all the money I made on the first business and was two weeks away from running out.

I started looking at jobs and wondered how we'd go about moving back to the city closest to where the jobs were.

I'd failed again.

This time it looked like there was no coming back.

My 7 Day Success

With two weeks left I had one last crack. This would be my final startup attempt.

I learned a lot from my first and second businesses and wanted to try to apply this knowledge to my new idea. This time, I didn't have seven years or eleven months. At the end of the week, I needed traction on the idea or I would have to shut everything down and start job hunting.

Running mainly on adrenaline, I ignored a lot of the activities I would typically spend time on when planning a business. Instead, I focused only on things that would lead to paying customers.

I avoided steps including:

- Sexy ideas. I wanted to solve a problem and sell a service. Fast.
- My failure. I had failed a lot in fourteen years, but I didn't have time to worry about my shortcomings.
- Permission. I used to ask for opinions on my ideas, but not this time.

- Assumptions. There was no time to make them or to test them. I had to launch.
- The small stuff. I didn't have months to agonize over a logo, business name or design—I put the site up in one day.
- Pricing strategy. I set a price and would let my customers tell me whether it was worth it.
- The perfect payment gateway. Informly's payment gateway took six months to set up. This time, I used a PayPal button that I set up in 30 minutes.

On Saturday, I decided to launch WP Live Ninja (now WP Curve), a WordPress support service that offered unlimited small WordPress jobs 24/7 for $69 per month. By Saturday afternoon the domain was registered; on Tuesday the site was live; and by Wednesday I sent out an email launching the service. I landed my first paying customer that day.

In the first week, I signed up 10 customers. This resulted in $476 of recurring monthly revenue, which was the exact amount I'd worked up to during the previous twelve months with Informly.

This may not sound like much, but my excitement was through the roof! This was the one and people were voting with their wallets. WordPress issues are an annoying problem that people are prepared to pay for. It was a monthly recurring service in a big market that I knew could scale into something significant.

Within twenty-three days I was covering costs and within a month my San Francisco-based co-founder Alex had joined me. Thoughts of moving to get a job were a distant memory.

Each month we grew by around 15% because people started proactively spreading the word. After 13 months we had 475 customers and were making over $33,000 in monthly recurring revenue (MRR). Just as important for me, I had blown past my $100,000 annual wage.

After one year, WP Curve was far ahead of where my agency was after seven. We had twice as many customers, twice the revenue, more staff, a stronger team, lower costs, a simpler business model, happier customers, and four times more profit.

Most importantly, it was a real business. A high growth startup in a big market with a lot of potential. We are still growing at 15%+ per month. After fourteen years, I'd finally realized my dream of being an entrepreneur running a high growth startup.

It only took 7 Days.

WHAT IS A STARTUP?

"A startup is a human institution designed to deliver a new product or service under conditions of extreme uncertainty."
Eric Ries

There is a lot of bullshit in startup land. Every second person is starting an incubator, raising money, pivoting, exiting, scaling, starting, failing, and telling the world as they do it.

That said, I do prefer the word "Startup" to the word "Business," which is why I've used it in this book.

A business is anything that derives a wage for its founder. By that definition, buying a lawn mowing franchise or opening a corner store is a business. But neither is a startup.

A startup is a bit more exciting. It has:

1. High impact potential
2. High levels of innovation
3. High levels of uncertainty

A local business can't be a startup without ambitions to take it to the world. A franchise restricted by franchise rules can't be a startup. Neither has the potential for a big impact.

Eric Ries defines a startup as *"a human institution designed to deliver a new product or service under conditions of extreme uncertainty."* That doesn't mean you have to risk everything to create a startup. This book is primarily about reducing risk. But with a startup you do lose some of the predictability and certainty that comes with less innovative businesses.

If there's no innovation, then it's not a startup. That's why the majority of startups have a technical focus. That said, innovation can also be present in ways other than with technology.

With high impact potential and high levels of innovation, a startup has the ability to change the world.

That's why I want you to think about launching a startup instead of a business. Anyone can create a job for themselves. But not everyone can change the world.

IDEA, EXECUTION, HUSTLE

"Things may come to those who wait ... but only the things left by those who hustle."
Anonymous

There is so much business advice out there that it's hard to cut through what's needed to get a startup going. Consider the following popular maxims:

- Work *on* your business, not *in* your business—impossible and impractical when you are bootstrapping a new idea.
- Optimize your funnel—pointless when you have no leads.
- Hack your growth—difficult before you have customers.

The goal of this book is to get you from wantrepreneur (someone who wants to be an entrepreneur) to entrepreneur. From someone who has an idea to someone who has a startup.

I chat with wantrepreneurs about their ideas all the time. Almost every time they are failing at one of three things, almost in equal measure. On the flip side, successful startup companies excel at all of them.

I can't think of a single entrepreneur that I've met who does all of these things well. This is part of the reason why the vast majority of successful startups are teams not individuals. Be honest with yourself. If you can't do all of these things alone, it's time to find a co-founder.

Idea

Another popular maxim in entrepreneurial circles is, “Ideas don’t matter, only execution matters.”

That advice is well-intentioned, but wrong.

Take a look at the trending startups on Angel List, the companies getting funded through Crunchbase, or think about your successful entrepreneurial friends. They are all working on something that has some sort of unique quality to it. It might not be the next iPhone, but it is an idea that has successfully captured enough attention to take off.

Your idea is important and I dedicate a fair amount of time to it on Day 1.

The problem is, it’s only one part of three elements required to successfully get a startup off the ground. It’s where wantrepreneurs spend 100% of their time. They can talk 'till they are blue in the face about their idea, but when it comes to the other elements, they fall flat.

We will spend one day on your idea, you will choose the best one, and then we'll move on.

Execution

Once you have an idea that has some merit, it needs to be executed well. This book is all about getting something to market quickly. However, that doesn't take away from the fact that it's an ongoing process to continually execute your idea well.

EXECUTION IS YOUR ABILITY TO PRESENT YOUR IDEA JUST AS WELL AS THE BEST IDEAS IN THE WORLD.

You won't be able to execute your idea in seven days at a level that compares with the best in the world. That should be your goal in the medium term.

There's no use complaining about being self-funded and not having resources. Customers don't care. They make comparisons and make a choice. If you don't execute as well as the competition, they will chose the competition.

Execution is a really big problem outside of the big startup hubs. It's very misunderstood, and simply getting a brand

and a website to look and feel like an exciting startup is difficult.

If you aren't able to present your idea in a way that compares favourably with the best in the world, then look for a co-founder who can.

Hustle

The final element is hustle. I'm not necessarily talking about cold calling or "getting out of the building."

HUSTLE IS RELENTLESSLY PURSUING WHAT NEEDS TO BE DONE AT THE TIME.

Hustle is Marco Zappacosta from Thumbtack getting a "No" from 42 out of 44 VCs.

Hustle is Seth Godin getting 900 rejection letters in a row.

Hustle is Chris Sacca creating a company, a website, and business cards just to be taken seriously at networking events.

Hustle for an early stage startup is generally about spending your time on the things that are most likely to bring you customers. That could mean "getting out of the building" for some. For you, your skillset, your customers, and your business, it might mean something totally different.

I built my business off the back of content marketing. I wrote 250 posts in the first year, 13 in one day. Our content is now a lead generation machine to the point where we don't advertise at all.

For you, it could be networking. It could be calling people and asking them to pay. It could be working on relationships. Whatever it is, it has to be the best way for you to spend your time, to solve your biggest problem right now.

If you don't yet have a business, you need to launch and this book will help you do that. You need to hustle for the next seven days and you can get it done. You have to *not* do the other stuff, and relentlessly pursue launching.

Once you launch, you need to get more people paying you. You have to relentlessly pursue your best method of getting customers, and not the stuff you naturally gravitate to.

Anti-hustle is what wantrepreneurs do. They do everything other than what *needs* to be done. They keep coding. They design new features. They optimize their site. They think up new, world-changing ideas. They hang out at startup events discussing their idea. They go to startup weekend and launch a new idea. They do everything other than what they need to do—which, more often than not, is getting more customers.

Some people are not good at hustle.

They don't know how to filter the noise, work out what they really need to do, and then tirelessly get that shit done.

Be honest with yourself. If idea, execution, or hustle are not you, then find a co-founder who excels in those areas. You will need it if you want to have a successful startup.

WHY 7 DAYS?

"Move fast and break things." **Mark Zuckerberg**

13 years into my soul-crushing indoctrination into entrepreneurship, it became clear why I'd failed so many times. I had acted based on assumptions instead of making decisions based on real data.

- When I purchased another company, I assumed I could bolt on $40,000 profit. Wrong.
- When I launched Informly, I assumed that if I created something great then people would buy it. Wrong.
- When I released a new version of Informly, I assumed that people would act according to the survey results. Wrong again.

The only time I didn't act out of assumptions was with WP Curve. I had no time to assume anything. I launched, and every important decision came afterwards. I based those decisions on real customer behavior, not assumptions.

The ability to learn from real data is why the 7 Day Startup works. You wipe assumptions off the table. Your focus is on launching in 7 Days.

Avoid Failed Validation Techniques

"The Lean Startup" movement has made people think that business has become a simple scientific experiment. Pre-sell $10,000 worth of your product and there's a definite need there. Create a landing page, and if you get conversions of over 30%, then you have a great business.

It's validated.

In rare circumstances, this works. Let's delve into some of the reasons why, in most cases, it doesn't.

Validation Doesn't Work Well When the Answer Isn't an Obvious "YES"

The popular stories you hear about startup validation go something like this:

1. I created a website with a brief video.
2. It went viral.
3. I bought a yacht.

Dropbox started from a 3-minute video posted to Hacker News and their signup list jumped to 75,000 people in one day. At the time of writing they are now a $10 billion company.

That's great *if* you can get 75,000 opt-ins in one day. But if you don't, is it a bad idea? Maybe you just don't have much kudos on Hacker News. Maybe people don't understand it. Maybe your video is crap. Maybe the right people didn't see it.

The reality is that most ideas aren't going to go viral. Let's face it: the chances of you coming up with the next Dropbox are low. This is particularly true for bootstrapped companies.

Email Opt-In/Beta Signup Totals Do Not Indicate Purchase Intent

Email signups are often considered the key indicator of whether an idea is sound.

With the first version of my analytics dashboard, I had 1,000 people sign up for the beta (three months) and 1,200 people enter their email to be notified of launch.

These may seem like small numbers, but it took five years to build up an email list of 2,000 people in my last business. I really felt like I was onto a winner.

There is a very big difference between someone entering their email and someone paying you each month for a product. I've consistently discovered that once I launch a product, on page conversions go down. It's easy for someone to enter their email to be notified.

It's much harder for someone to sign up, try, and use a new service.

People Saying "It's a Good Idea" Doesn't Mean It Is

As part of validating Buffer, Joel Gascoigne "simply tweeted the link and asked people what they thought of the idea."

His post on validating Buffer indicates that he read a lot into this:

> *"After a few people used it to give me their email and I got some useful feedback via email and Twitter, I considered it validated. In the words of Eric Ries, I had my first validated learning about customers."*

Really? A few of your mates said it was a good idea and therefore it's "validated?"

It turns out that Buffer *was* a good idea and a product that people were willing to pay for. Does that mean the validation technique was a good one? I don't think so.

Here are some of the things that people around me said when I built Informly:

- *"It's a great business."* (Startup veteran Jason Calacanis. I sent him a login; he never logged in).
- *"I'm not sure if this email will make it to you, but you've managed to build the software most of us wished we already did!"* (Startup founder and angel investor; didn't end up becoming a paid customer).

- *"Thanks for helping to solve a problem most of us face every day,"* and *"Great work man! I use this product frequently and have recommended it to quite a few people."* (Didn't end up becoming a paid customer).
- *"I have just jumped onto the new platform from http://inform.ly and love it!"* (Didn't end up becoming a paid customer).
- *"I'm in love with it. Let me know if you ever need a testimonial. I've been waiting for this all my life".* (Didn't end up becoming a paid customer).
- *"Hey Dan! Informly is amazing! What an epic idea. You can manage everything that matters from one place"* (Didn't end up becoming a paid customer).

These are unsolicited. I had a lot of friends telling me it was a great idea and also giving me great testimonials. They are bad at predicting their own behavior and even if they think they will buy, it doesn't mean they will.

People don't want to hurt your feelings.

Coverage in Tech Press Doesn't Work

When I launched the first version of Informly it was a personal validation goal to get featured by a respected tech publication. I thought having that level of confirmation would be some sort of indication that I was onto something.

So I was thrilled to get coverage with The Next Web and Mashable, and Australian tech sites like Startup Daily, Anthill, and StartupSmart. This was pretty remarkable given that:

- I'd never built a consumer web app before.
- I had marketed it mainly through my own blog posts.
- When I started I had no network in the startup community.
- I had no funding and no co-founders.

I've read stories of getting 12,000 users from Mashable coverage. Combine that with the other coverage, and I should be onto a winner, right? Guess how many paid users were sent by the above traffic sources?

Zero.

Targeted Surveys Don't Work

I know which content...		
	Total	**Percentage**
Views & engagement	28	37%
Social shares	20	26%
Leads	9	12%
Revenue	4	5%
People	4	5%
Would pay		
Yes	17	22%
No	16	21%
Possibly	43	57%

Not long after realizing that the idea wasn't going to fly, I decided to pivot to a content marketing analytics app. This time I was determined to make sure I validated the idea before working on it for six months.

I built a targeted list of keen content marketers and asked them a bunch of questions in a survey. The purpose of the survey was to ascertain:

- Were people measuring their content marketing?
- Would they pay for a tool that enabled them to measure it?

It even included specific questions like "Would you pay for this feature if I built it?" The results are above and they are clear:

- People generally weren't measuring the important metrics for working out if their content was resulting in more business.
- 60% would possibly pay for it.
- 20% would definitely pay for it.

I thought it was tapping into a big need.

Post launch, most of the people in the beta list didn't even use the product. No one paid for it and, after launching it to the public, the signup rate (on-page conversions) was well below the previous version of the product.

Three people signed up to pay for this new iteration. One cancelled within a week and the other two didn't actually use it.

I should blame the product for some of this. It was the best I could do within six weeks and it definitely needed improvement. But the results were shocking to me at the time. How could they be so different from the survey results?

As Steve Jobs said, "*People don't know what they want until you show it to them.*" The opposite is also true:

PEOPLE DON'T KNOW WHAT THEY DON'T WANT UNTIL THEY ARE FORCED TO OPEN THEIR WALLETS.

Pre-Selling is a Flawed Experiment

Pre-selling your product before it exists is often touted as the answer to startup validation techniques that don't work. This is how pre-selling works.

- You make an offer for people to pre-purchase your product at a discount.
- People are getting a good deal, but since the product isn't live yet, they accept that they might have to wait a while and are happy to make that compromise.

There are a few reasons why this approach is often not the way to go:

- Your goal at this stage in the business is to test your assumptions. Making overly generous offers is only testing whether or not someone wants to pay you the heavily discounted amount. It doesn't test your real offer and is therefore a flawed experiment.

- People get excited about launches. Time and time again I get higher conversions on pre-launch pages than I do once products actually launch. The same applies to pre-selling. Just because you can get a few people to sign up for your "coming soon business," it doesn't validate the business. You may find after you launch that you have no momentum to continue building the business. In that respect it might be a useful way to fund your idea, but it's not a method of validation.
- The people who sign up to pre-sold deals may be your best customers. By providing them with a yearly (or god forbid lifetime) plan, you have killed any chance of building momentum with those people as you grow. Momentum is a key part of a successful startup. Countless businesses have died after an over-hyped launch and a failure to build ongoing traction.

The idea of someone paying you actual money *before* you build something has a lot of appeal, but you have to ask yourself what you are testing. To *really* test whether you can build a business, you have to start building it.

A few one off sales doesn't get you any closer to knowing whether you can do that.

The Concept of "Validation" is Too Simplistic

The fact is, business isn't some sort of simple scientific experiment. There are a lot of factors that influence whether your company will thrive or die. "Validated" implies that it will be a good business, but there are a lot more influencing factors.

Luck plays a huge part. Timing might even be more important. The abilities to sell your great idea or build a team to execute your idea are also important factors. There's a huge forgotten void between "idea" and "successful business" that validation doesn't account for.

A lot of the ideas that people have are great ideas that are already validated. If someone is doing the exact same thing you are doing and doing it successfully, then the idea is valid, right? Maybe; but does that mean you can create a successful business with the same idea? Not necessarily.

Again, this is particularly true for bootstrapped founders with limited resources. “Validated” doesn’t mean the business will work. Achieving “product market fit” doesn’t mean the business will work.

Product/market/founder fit is probably more useful, but I’m beginning to sound like a university assignment. We’re living in the land of assumptions.

No more assumptions. No more validation. Launch.

Work More Efficiently

When I was at university I figured out that I worked much faster the day before my assignments were due. At first I fought it because it seemed like a slack student thing to do. By the end, I embraced it.

When an assignment was announced, I would go to the library and copy ten or so books that were relevant to the topic. I wouldn't touch the assignment again until the day before it was due. That's when I'd crack open the books and delve into the content. For exams, it meant I was more likely to remember the content the next day and my work rate was insanely efficient.

This strategy took me from failing three out of four subjects in my first year to averaging six and a half out of seven in my last year. They even put me on the Dean's list for exceptional students. If only the Dean knew!

You don't want to do this every night, but there's no doubt that a kick in the arse will drive you—at least temporarily—to perform at a higher level.

It's proven in research. You work more efficiently when you are close to a deadline. If you are a long way out, you make tasks up that you think are important. As a result, you don't get any of the important work done.

Before you start a task, your brain visualizes the hardest parts to come. It then tries to simulate real work by focusing on small mindless tasks. In other words, you spend hours and days fussing over logos and website copy instead of selling your product!

Once you start something with a clear end date, it drives you forward.

Be an Entrepreneur

A wantrepreneur is someone who wants to be an entrepreneur, but is so obsessed with watching TED talks and talking about their business ideas that they never launch them.

You know the type? Every time you see them, they have a new million dollar idea. Or a sad story about how they thought of Facebook three years before Zuckerberg.

They don't understand that entrepreneurs are rarely the inventors who came up with breakthrough technologies. Instead, they are people who took a small problem and worked it to death until they found a solution that gained traction.

IF YOU HAVE A CONVERSATION WITH A FRIEND ABOUT YOUR BUSINESS IDEA THIS MONTH, AND NEXT MONTH YOU ARE HAVING THE SAME CONVERSATION, YOU ARE A WANTREPRENEUR.

If you want to be an entrepreneur, you have to launch. If you follow the ideas in this book, I believe you can become an entrepreneur by this time next week.

But 7 Days is Not Long Enough

Yes it is.

It's amazing what you can achieve in 7 Days. You can't deliver on your whole grand vision, but you can launch something. When you do, you can start talking to people who are paying you money. This is when you start making sensible business decisions and avoid assumptions.

Beware that launching fast requires you to compromise a lot.

Once you commit to launching in 7 Days, you'll change your thinking on exactly what to launch.

In this book, I'll run through examples from all sorts of companies that have been able to launch in 7 Days. These cover a wide range including services, software, product delivery and marketplaces. Not just all businesses you would associate with quick and easy launches.

Still not convinced?

- Is your business in non-professional services or consulting? You can call someone right now, help them, and ask for money.
- Do you want to launch a plugin or software app? What can you do manually instead of with the software—at least in the short term? What features can you live without? Start talking with real paying customers and use those conversations to decide on your next move.
- Are you looking to release an online training or membership site? The technology will allow you to launch it in 7 Days. Save your epic launch plans for later, when you can make decisions based on real customer behavior.
- Want to create a physical product? How about you sell someone else's product first and get real feedback instead of acting on assumptions?

People who start businesses in these fields take months or years to plan and execute it, only to learn that it wasn't a good business to start with.

Launching in 7 Days requires a mindset shift. In the past, a software app like the one described above would go into an incubator and get seed funding. The founders would build a team and work on the product for six months before launching. But what happens if it's not a hit? They pivot to figure out why and try to work out how much of their wasted code they can salvage.

The 7 Day Startup mindset is that you will launch it in 7 Days. You won't waste any time building something that you don't know people want.

Once you aim for a week, you will start to question every assumption and figure out a way to make it happen.

No. Seriously. I Can't Launch in 7 Days.

If that really is the case then perhaps you are going about it the wrong way. If you have launched a dozen successful businesses, and you are doing it for fun, let's face it: you probably don't need this book. If not, what you need is to minimize risk and minimize the time you spend working based on assumptions.

If your idea is going to take six months to test, then I would suggest choosing a different idea. This book will help you do that.

Let's get stuck in. It's time to launch a startup!

The 7 Pre-Launch Tasks

This is not like a typical business book. Don't bother with tactics to "find your ideal market" or "create your unique selling proposition" or "practice your elevator pitch." These activities are pointless before you launch because they are based on assumptions.

I will walk you through exactly what to do on each of the 7 Days. For now, let's consider the things that need to happen before you launch.

> **Day One** - You need to have an idea. I'll explain how to generate ideas and tell a good one from a bad one (as best we can without having real customers).
> **Day Two** - You need to have something to launch at the end of the seven days. I'll explain what a Minimum Viable Product (MVP) is and you can start thinking about what you will launch.
> **Day Three** - You need a business name. It doesn't really matter what it is, but I'll look at a few ways you can create a simple, useful name.

Day Four - You need a landing page or some sort of online presence. I'll show you how to build a website in less than a day.

Day Five - In this chapter I will give you a look at free methods for getting your business in front of enough people to help you decide whether or not to continue.

Day Six - You need to measure what success means to you. The last thing you want is to launch and then not know whether you have a hit a few weeks later. I'll help you set some goals and plan to make changes if you don't reach those goals.

Day Seven - You have to launch.

In the last chapter, "Business Rules to Live By" I will outline the general principles that you can apply to any business.

If you were expecting a 50-page plan, I'm sorry to disappoint.

You can use these steps when launching your business or any product within a current business. I'm assuming you are launching an entire business, so please keep that in mind as you read the chapters.

Note you will also have to go through a process at some stage to set up a legal entity. As I'm not a lawyer, I can't tell you whether you have to do that before you launch. I won't be discussing the legal aspects of setting up a business in this book.

Play Along on Twitter

I'm really keen to play along as you build your business. Give me a shout out on Twitter with the hashtag #7daystartup (my handle is @thedannorris) as you go, and let me know what you are up to. Or if you prefer, feel free to email me at dan@wpcurve.com.

THE 7 DAY STARTUP

Day 1 - The 9 Elements of a Great Bootstrapped Business Idea

"The world always seems brighter when you've just made something that wasn't there before." **Neil Gaiman**

As I've previously mentioned, it's not helpful or accurate to suggest that ideas don't matter.

There are a lot of things that matter in making a successful business:

1. **The Idea Matters** - A bad idea, executed well, will not make a good business.

2. **Execution Matters** - A good idea, executed poorly, will not make a good business.
3. **A Founder's Ability to Get Customers (To Hustle) Matters** - A great idea, executed well, will fail without customers.
4. **Timing Matters** - Speaking hypothetically about an idea is pointless if the timing is wrong.
5. **Luck Matters** - In fact, it matters much more than most entrepreneurs would care to admit.

Your idea matters. At the same time, you don't want to stress over it for weeks on end. In fact, you should spend just one day on it.

The beauty is that you can always change your idea once you start learning from real customer data. This isn't politics. Backflips are highly encouraged in Startup Land!

If you only spend one day on your idea, you'll be more open to changing it if doesn't work out.

You might already have some ideas—you might hear people complaining about a pain point, or you might have to start cold-calling people to find out what you can work on. I can't give you the idea for your next business.

An idea that you think is great or that someone tells you is great may not result in a good business for you.

The 9 Elements of a Bootstrapped Business Idea

1. Enjoyable daily tasks

You often hear people say "follow your passion" when it comes to business. Thankfully, I learned early on that this is a bad idea. When I was younger I did a trial for a mechanics apprenticeship. I aced the exam, prompting the manager to ask me why I wanted to be a mechanic. I told him I was "passionate" about cars. He said, "So is Jay Leno, but he doesn't fix cars for a living".

If you want to be an entrepreneur, you need to be passionate about growing a business.

I've also made the mistake of starting businesses that I flat out didn't like. This is a motivation killer that has to be avoided.

Rather than complicating things with diagrams and rules, let's just agree on this:

IT MAKES NO SENSE TO START A BUSINESS THAT IS GOING TO HAVE YOU DOING WORK YOU DON'T ENJOY.

That's as far as we need to take the passion equation.

Think long and hard about what your day-to-day tasks will be. Visualize yourself doing these tasks.

If you don't like what you see, then it's not a good business idea for you. Other than that, don't worry about passion.

2. Product/founder fit

People talk a lot about product/market fit, but for bootstrappers the idea of product/founder fit is just as important. In my first agency, I was a poor match. I knew that, but I pushed on anyway.

Some people are perfectly matched with their companies and some people aren't. It's worth thinking about what skills you have, what are you known for, and where you can provide the most value.

If that doesn't line up with your business idea, then it's going to be a long, hard struggle.

3. Scalable business model

For listed companies, if profits unexpectedly go up, the stock explodes. If they unexpectedly fall, the stock crashes. This is because businesses rarely stagnate. It's considered unusual if a business is neither growing or contracting.

Yet freelancers and small business people accept a business that isn't growing. They accept that the business barely generates a wage for the founder.

Startup founders should have the ambition to grow their business into a larger company. If you don't have that ambition, what you are creating is not a startup.

Some businesses lend themselves to business models that have growth in their DNA. A software as a service (SaaS) company would expect to bring in more recurring revenue each month. A local store or a franchise, however, will have fairly static (albeit cyclical) profits.

Your idea is not a solid startup idea if you don't have the capacity to make use of a profitable, growing business model.

It's time to start thinking about how you might charge consumers and whether you could reasonably expect to grow this business idea month over month.

4. Operates profitably without the founder

Most small businesses would die without their founders. They are too tied to the delivery of the product or service, or they just don't have enough profits to hire people to replace all of the jobs they do.

A lot of people fall into the trap of not worrying about this because they expect to "hustle" early on with little reward. It's okay to accept that, but fundamentally there needs to be a profit margin built into the product or service you sell.

You need to be able to see a point where you can hire in staff or systems to replace you, and still continue to generate a profit. At that point it becomes a real business.

Can you see your idea becoming a real business that operates profitably without you?

5. An asset you can sell

Business is not just about making money. It's about creating something that is valuable. Not "I think what I'm doing is valuable," but a third party validating that there is value there.

Things that carry value are assets, so it's your job as a startup founder to build them.

FOCUSING ON SHORT-TERM LAUNCHES OR PROJECTS WON'T BUILD ASSETS. ASSETS ARE BUILT OVER TIME BY IGNORING SHORT-TERM DISTRACTIONS IN FAVOR OF A BIGGER, LONG-TERM VISION.

A list of customers that pay you every month is an asset. If you focus on short-term projects you'll make more money initially. But if you turn down projects and focus on providing recurring value, you build a valuable asset.

Your product design and intellectual property are assets. If you resell or copy someone else's product, you might have better margins in the short term; but creating your own gives you a long-term asset.

Your team is an asset. If you hire mediocre people to save money, you get more money in the short term. If you hire great people, you are building a valuable asset that grows your business.

Your website is an asset. If you pay cheap SEO teams to spam your site with crap, you might rank in Google for one day. But if you deliver outstanding content for years, you'll end up with an unbeatable competitive advantage.

Traffic to your website is great, but a large list of people on your email list is an asset.

At the idea stage you have to think about what assets your idea will result in. Some ideas—when worked on—will naturally result in the development of assets over time, and some won't.

If you work on this idea for five years, what will you have in the end?

6. Large market potential

The long-term goal of a startup is to become a legitimate player in the industry and create an impact. To do that, they have to serve large markets. They may start serving a small market, but to maintain consistently growing profits, they can't be restricted by the pool they are swimming in.

At the idea stage, give some thought to whether you are building a business for a small group of people or whether it can grow into a large market.

7. Tap into pain or pleasure differentiators

Everyone will tell you to have a "unique selling proposition" or a "differentiator." What they don't tell you is it's not enough to just be different.

All that matters is what your customers care about.

WP Curve is not just unique compared to competitors. It also goes above and beyond in the areas that matter most to customers.

- Our support is unlimited, so customers don't have to worry about the pain of unexpected invoices.
- Our support is live 24/7, so customers don't have to worry about the pain of being organized and waiting around for advice.

- We offer same day turnaround on jobs, so customers can enjoy the pleasure of creating new content on their site, instead of waiting around for days or weeks to have it fixed.

I'd worked with small business owners for many years and I knew the agency model just didn't cut it anymore. The industry went from web developers being the only one to touch a website to business owners maintaining their own content in a few short years. Agencies weren't equipped to deal with this and provide the service that the new type of business owner needed.

The technical change had resulted in a different set of expectations for customers. Agencies failing to meet those expectations had created a new set of pain points for customers. Our service solved those pain points.

What will your customers really care about? Does your idea tap into a deep pain or pleasure point for them? Or is it just 'a cool idea'?

8. Unique lead generation advantage

As I mentioned above, having a good idea that is executed well isn't the full equation. You still need to find customers. The best bootstrapped businesses have ways of generating leads that tap into a key differentiator in the business or the founder.

For example, CrazyEgg and KissMetrics generate a huge percentage of their business through content marketing. Their co-founder, Neil Patel, is probably the most prolific creator of high quality content in the industry. This is a unique advantage for Neil's companies.

John Dumas from Entrepreneur on Fire is a confident and energetic presenter. He has generated six-figure months in his first year of business by selling directly on webinars. This way of generating leads taps into a core skill that gives John his advantage.

How you are going to generate leads for your business? What will make you, and your company, unique?

9. Ability to launch quickly

Unfortunately, innovations like the iPhone don't get built by first-time entrepreneurs or self-funded companies. For a business idea to be a good idea for a bootstrapper, it needs to be something you can launch quickly.

Complex software products, physical products, or local physical businesses are difficult. If it's going to take you a year to launch, you won't learn from real customer data as you go.

Choose an idea that you can launch and modify quickly. Then when you start getting real data from paying customers, you can innovate and get the product just right.

I'd love it if you chose something that you can launch in seven days. If you can't, you should still pick an idea you can launch in two months as opposed to two years.

Is Your Idea a Good Idea?

Consider most small businesses. It's clear that they don't meet many of the above elements.

- They don't generate enough profit to pay a replacement founder, and when they do, it's not consistent.
- They are difficult to sell for a reasonable amount of money. If you are able to sell them, they might fall apart without the founder.
- They die because one piece fails or they often hit ceilings where they can't grow anymore.
- Their revenue plateaus year after year because they operate in small markets.

Think about your own idea and whether it's going to fall into the same traps. Choose a business idea that meets the nine elements well and you are ready to move on.

You can tweak the idea later, but some of these fundamentals will be hard issues to solve later on. It's important that the potential is there from the start. You should also consider these things:

Don't Pick Low-Hanging Fruit

Creating a startup means creating something valuable for your customers that is a long-term asset. It doesn't mean going after low-hanging fruit, getting caught up in get rich quick schemes, or chasing passive income. Here are some examples:

- Web designers host client sites to make a bit of money. The host is delivering the most value in that scenario.
- Consultants "white label" existing products and double the price. What value are they creating? What asset are they building?
- Drop shippers take someone else's products and sell them for more money without doing much. This is okay for the short term, but what separates them from everyone else? Their Google rankings? Good luck with that.

We are talking about launching a real startup here. Something that gives you a purpose, creates something original in the world, and builds long term value. You need to think about how you can truly create something.

Consistently producing original concepts will boost your motivation and confidence, set you up as an authority, and put you in a place where you can develop real, long-term assets.

Creating something real could mean writing content on your company blog, or producing a software app that accomplishes a task slightly better than everyone else. You could start a services business that delivers services in a unique way. Or make a physical product that offers something new.

It *is* possible to start a business without constructing anything, but in the long term the businesses that stand out are the most creative ones.

Creation doesn't just happen one day in the future when you think the time is right.

It's something that the best companies and the smartest entrepreneurs do every day.

It took me seven years to build my agency "business," and only after selling it did I realize that it wasn't a real business. I want you to build a real business the first time.

It needs to be original and provide significant, ongoing value to its customers; and to you.

Don't Try to be Steve Jobs

With Informly, I tried to be Steve Jobs.

I let my creative side take over my entrepreneurial side. It helps for entrepreneurs to be creative, but fundamentally entrepreneurship is about creating a product that people want and selling it to them.

Jobs' statement, "*People don't know what they want until you show it to them,*" is correct. It's also extremely dangerous advice for a new entrepreneur. Informly ultimately failed. I'm not Steve Jobs.

PLAYING THE VISIONARY IS A PRIVILEGE RESERVED FOR SECOND-AND THIRD-TIME ENTREPRENEURS. IT'S FUN, BUT IT'S FRAUGHT WITH DANGER.

As an entrepreneur you need something that people want to pay for, with their money or attention. Asking them will not work, because people are bad at predicting their own behavior.

For your first startup, there is a much easier way:

SOLVE PROBLEMS WHERE PEOPLE ARE ALREADY PAYING FOR SOLUTIONS.

Compare my analytics dashboard software to our WordPress support service. Customers generally used Google Analytics (which is free). Most didn't use paid analytics software and didn't even know that you could get dashboards with all of your stats in the one place.

I was trying to establish a new behavior and convince them of a problem they didn't know they had.

For WP Curve, most of the people in our audience use WordPress. They aren't developers, which means from time to time they will run into problems. To varying degrees, most of them were paying to solve these problems either by:

- Engaging an agency (an expensive option, creating a pain point around cost).
- Using a freelancer (who is only one person and isn't always available, creating a pain point around responsiveness).

- Finding cheap developers on marketplace sites (creating pain points around security, quality of work, and lack of project management).

We could relieve these pain points without cultivating any new behaviors from our customers. They are already budgeting for it and resigned to the fact that they have to pay for it.

Thinking about your business this way can be useful, even at the idea stage.

EVERYONE MIGHT BE SAYING THAT YOUR IDEA IS GREAT, BUT LOOK AT WHETHER OR NOT THEY ARE CURRENTLY PAYING FOR A SOLUTION TO THE SAME PROBLEM.

This will tell you how hard it will be to convince them to pay you for your product.

When you've had a few exits and you've bought the yacht, it's time to be Steve Jobs.

Until then, start by solving existing problems that people are already paying for solutions to.

Idea Evaluation Checklist

The Nine Elements	Comment
Enjoyable daily tasks	
Product/founder fit	
Scalable business model	
Operates profitably without the founder	
An asset you can sell	
Large market potential	
Taps into pain or pleasure differentiators	
Unique lead generation advantage	
Ability to launch quickly	

Day 1 Task - *Brainstorm a bunch of ideas and evaluate them against the checklist. Choose the idea that stands out as being the best option for you. You can use the template provided at wpcurve.com/7daystartup if that helps.*

Day 2 - WTF is an MVP?

"Learning is the essential unit of progress for startups."
Eric Ries

The Lean Startup introduced a lot of new fancy words into startup lingo. The most misunderstood is the MVP, or "Minimum Viable Product."

The concept of the MVP is (in Eric Ries' words):

> *"The first step is to enter the Build phase as quickly as possible with a minimum viable product (MVP). The MVP is that version of the product that enables a full turn of the Build-Measure-Learn loop with a minimum amount of effort and the least amount of development time."*

What this means: Rather than spending six months creating a product or service, do only the smallest amount of work required to truly test it.

In practice, this is interpreted in a lot of ways that prove to be detrimental to bootstrapped startups. They create a really crappy version of the product or service without enough features to make it desirable enough for someone to pay for. Or they don't create anything, and instead put up a landing page and base their decisions on email opt-ins. Or they realize it will take too long to create their actual product, so they create something else.

Most of these interpretations go wrong when they get away from effectively measuring what needs to be measured. In short, they overemphasize the "minimum" and underemphasize the "viable."

A COMMON MVP MISTAKE IS OVER-EMPHASIZING THE "MINIMUM" AND UNDER-EMPHASIZING THE "VIABLE."

As an example, Informly was designed to pull in people's stats and give them a summary. I wanted to test if people wanted to pay for this, so I built out a working version with only a few integrations. Most startup founders would call this an MVP.

Yet this fails the MVP test. Why?

I put out a product with a lot fewer features than other products that were already available. As a result, no one wanted it. Does that mean it was a bad idea or the business was doomed? There was no way to tell. If it did have all the features, it may have been more popular.

A much better MVP would have been:

1. Put screenshots up of an analytics report and explain what the product does.
2. When someone signs up (pays), get them to click on a few logos to select the services they liked.
3. Tell them their report will be ready soon.
4. Call them up and talk them through what's being done, build the report, and give it to them.

This would have taken me one day.

It would have tested my assumption that people wanted the service much more effectively than a feature-lacking product. The customer would have experienced something reasonably similar to what my product would do for them.

Once you have your product or service idea, it's time to think about what you can launch within one week that represents your final vision for your product or service as closely as possible. That is from the customer's point of view. The ugly "behind the scenes" view does not matter right now.

The key is to forget about automation and figure out what you can do manually.

The WP Curve MVP

I didn't make the same mistake twice with WP Curve because I had no choice but to make it happen in a week. If I had longer, I may have started looking at support systems or built one that suited our style of small jobs.

I might have started building out models for how developers would complete tasks or a WordPress plugin for requesting fixes. I probably would have hired developers around the world to make sure I could staff the business 24/7.

I didn't need to do any of that because there are manual replacements for all of it. This allowed me to give the exact service to the customer that I planned to give once we were established.

Here's how it looked:

1. I had a subscription to some live chat software left over from Informly, so I put that up on the site as the way to request jobs. It was available to everyone, not just customers, but I wasn't worried about that. If it wasted a bit of time, that was okay.
2. I only had one developer, which meant someone else had to be online the other 16 hours in the day. That was me. I had my phone on every night, running the live chat software. Anyone who jumped on chat in those early days was waking me up, but they didn't know it! Again, short-term pain was not a problem.
3. There was no time for a support desk so we used the live chat and a support email address. Customers didn't care; they prefer email.

This looks ugly as hell from a business owner's end. The customer, however, saw a developer on call 24/7, and they were validating the value of it by paying me.

An MVP in a service business isn't too hard, but with software or physical products it becomes a bit trickier. The same principles apply, though. You need to think about how you can mimic the customer experience as much as possible, as quickly as possible.

Here are a few examples of well-executed MVPs that went on to make great companies.

AppSumo

Noah Kagan wanted to make a deals site for software apps. He could have focused on building the platform for managing the deals or building the email list. Neither of those things were necessary to give customers a realistic taste of the product he had in mind.

Noah's vision was to provide customers with time-limited, heavily-discounted deals on digital goods. He was active on Reddit and found that Imgur was selling pro accounts on the site for $25 per year.

He emailed the founder of Imgur and asked him if he could sell the plan for a decent discount. He then bought a bunch of very affordable ads and sold 200 deals. It lacked all of the fancy systems that AppSumo has today, but to the customer it was very much in line with what you experience now.

In one weekend he was able to see that he had a way to market the idea, people would pay, and he could make money. AppSumo was a $1m company within one year.

Underground Cellar

Jeffrey Shaw wanted to build a daily deals website for wine with a twist. Instead of offering discounted deals, he would offer a randomized free upgrade with every purchase.

He assumed that the motivation for buying on the site would be about the excitement and surprise as opposed to the cost savings. The way he tested this was brilliant and represented a creative (and valid) MVP.

He threw a party!

Everyone who came paid $15 and got a bottle of wine. Some were $15 bottles, some were $100 bottles. Everyone loved the excitement of checking out what they got, particularly the ones with $100 bottles! People passed them around and chatted about the wines.

The actual business would have needed a custom website platform, a randomization technology, payment gateways, and much more. Jeff needed to know whether or not people would go for this concept. He was able to test it without any technology.

Undergroundcellar.com[10] was born and is now a profitable and established business.

Bare Metrics

The Baremetrics.io[11] story is one I love because Josh started something that was very similar to Informly, but he didn't make the same mistakes.

Josh Pigford was a user of the popular payment gateway Stripe and was desperate to get some decent analytics from his account. He had the idea in October 2013 and he built the first version in eight days.

He focused only on what he needed to make it worth paying for. He didn't overthink the details on the design or

---

10 "Underground Cellar," *Underground Cellar*, accessed August 23, 2014, https://www.undergroundcellar.com/.

11 Josh Pigford, "Baremetrics - Stripe Analytics & Metrics," *Baremetrics*, accessed July 21, 2014, https://baremetrics.io/

the development. His sole focus was to "get this to a point where I can prove people want it," and the only "proof" that is valid is money. As soon as it was remotely valuable, he shipped it.

He didn't ship a free version for people to play with. He shipped a working version and charged for it. After a month he was making $1,000 in MRR. Over the next few months, he continued to learn from paying customers, focusing on what they wanted (and ignoring the rest). After nine months he was earning $18,800 MRR.

When Josh launched, Bare Metrics was a limited feature set, but it did what it promised. Bare Metrics included a handful of metrics that you couldn't get from Stripe directly. It didn't allow you to set the date or deep dive into data and only updated once a day. But Bare Metrics was enough for people to want to pay for their services.

Josh's five lessons were:

1. Build what you need, not what you think others need (i.e. don't act on assumptions)
2. Charge from day one
3. Stop trying to build the perfect product

4. Ship fast, ship frequently
5. Price for the customers you want

Bare Metrics is a fairly simple analytics tool. However, their plans range from $29 to $249/month. This might rule some people out, but it also means his customers are serious businesses.

Tidy

Everyone knows two-sided marketplaces are one of the hardest business models to pull off, right? Well Stacey Jacobs didn't get the memo. After deciding to start a home cleaning marketplace, she built the site, engaged the cleaners, started marketing and had her first customers in seven days.

What I love about Stacey's story is she only did what was 100% necessary at each stage. For example, to get the supply side of the marketplace sorted (the cleaners), she didn't start a huge drive for signups. She simply put an ad on a classifieds site, narrowed the 60 replies down to 10 people to interview, and chose three. Three cleaners was enough for her to be able to offer the service in one region in Sydney's eastern suburbs.

To get customers, she ran enough online ads to sign up a few paying customers. She then focused on making them happy and getting them referring before moving on.

Stacy is operating in a space where similar companies, like HomeJoy, are landing multiple eight-figure investment rounds and deals with the likes of AirBnb. That doesn't mean she can't take a lean approach, launch quickly, and with minimal risk.

What Will Your MVP Look Like?

Today you need to think about what your MVP will look like and how you can build it in 7 Days. Here are some questions that you need to answer:

- How can you perform a service or offer a product to real customers?
- How will you get them to pay you after seven days?
- How close will your MVP be to the final vision of your product?
- What can you do manually (hint: probably everything)?
- What can you do yourself instead of delegating?

- How can you make your offer as real as possible for the end customer?

Your product or service will need to be at a point where you can offer it at the end of the week. This won't be easy. It will be fun. It will also force you to be creative and to put something in the hands of your customers and to ask them for money.

Day 2 Task - *Write down exactly what you will launch on Day 7. What will your customers get, what is included, and what is excluded? If necessary, write down what is automated and what will be done manually in the short term.*

Day 3 - Choose a Business Name

"It's more effective to do something valuable than to hope a logo or name will say it for you."
Jason Cohen (founder of WP Engine)

The purpose of the 7 Day Startup is to help you get to launch quickly and avoid the activities that are common distractions for early companies. There is no better example of this than choosing a business name, something that new entrepreneurs agonize over for weeks or months prior to launching.

There are a number of reasons why you don't need to spend more than a day on your business name:

1. It will distract you from what is really important, which is creating something great. That is ultimately what matters and will be what makes or breaks your brand.
2. Your business will probably change significantly by the time you get established. Nintendo started out making playing cards. Tiffany's started out making stationery.

3. You will grow into whatever name you come up with. Most names mean very little when they are first conceived. Steve Jobs impulsively named Apple after the farm he dropped acid on. If that method works, then anything goes!
4. You can change your business name down the track—often quite easily. Even big brands have managed to do so successfully. For small, agile startups, it can often be done for virtually zero cost in a matter of hours or days. You are not stuck with your name for life. Google started out as "BackRub." Creepy.
5. Your customers don't care.

Let's look at a useful framework for choosing an "acceptable" business name. This is the highest level you need to strive for at this stage in your business. Having the perfect worldwide brand can come later, but we want to avoid having a terrible name.

The irony is that a terrible name is often the result of overthinking it.

Come up With a Few Options

The most sensible way to approach your business name is to come up with a few options. From there you can use some logic to pick the best one.

There are many ways you might go about doing this. Here are some naming tricks to get started:

- A place. Apple was named after an apple farm. Adobe was named after a creek that ran behind the founder's house.
- Combine two words to create a new one. Aldi is a combination of "Albrecht" (name of the founders) and "discount." Intel combined "Integrated Electronics." Groupon combined "Group Coupon."
- Use an acronym for your service. IBM stood for "International Business Machines."
- Look for industry terms. In our case, "WP" is commonly used for companies in the WordPress space.
- Use the dictionary. Jack Dorsey liked the name Twitch so he looked at words around it in the dictionary and found the word "Twitter."
- Extend a related word. I put "inform" into wordoid.com to come up with Informly.

- Outsource it. crowdSPRING.com[12] is one site that will get others to come up with business names for you. The one-day turnaround might be an issue here, so forums or social media might work better, or you can ask your friends.

The more time you spend looking at names, the weirder it gets. IKEA was named after the first two letters of the founder's name (Ingvar Kamprad[13]) and the names of the property and the village in which he grew up (Elmtaryd Agunnaryd). Zynga was named after Mark Pincus' bulldog.

Yahoo started as "Jerry's Guide to the World Wide Web" and then became an acronym for "Yet Another Hierarchical Officious Oracle."

Where the name comes from doesn't really matter.

---

12 "Logo Design, Web Design and Naming by the World's Best Creative Team | crowdSPRING," *crowdSPRING*, accessed July 21, 2014, http://www.crowdspring.com/.

13 "Ingvar Kamprad," *Wikipedia*, last modified July 5, 2014, http://en.wikipedia.org/wiki/Ingvar_Kamprad/.

Come up with ten names that aren't ridiculous and then apply this framework to choose the best one.

A Framework for Choosing an Acceptable Business Name

1. Is it taken?

It's best not to choose a name that's already taken. I can't provide legal advice here on how to work out if you have the right to use a name, but as a bare minimum you should check:

- Is there a trademark on the name in your region? You can use uspto.gov/trademarks[14] in the U.S.
- Is the .com taken for the name? This will often point you to whether or not someone is actively using the name. This doesn't necessarily mean you rule it out, but it's another consideration.
- Is the Twitter handle taken? This can give you a good idea of how active someone is if the name is taken.

14 "Trademarks Home," *The United States Patent and Trademark Office*, last modified March 31, 2014, http://www.uspto.gov/trademarks/.

You can use knowem.com[15] to see what social profiles are active under the name.

- Are you able to register the name for your business in your local area?

None of these are absolute deal-breakers. There are plenty of businesses who have started with names that have been used for other things. It's up to you to look at how the name is being used and decide if it's an acceptable level of risk for you to use it.

2. Is it simple?

Always favor a name that's simple. Even if it doesn't mean anything, being simple makes it memorable. Eventually it will mean something. Case in point: Apple.

Here are some quick guidelines: Try to avoid making up words. Don't use misspellings or words that people commonly misspell. This only increases the chance people won't find you. Most importantly, keep your name to fewer

15 "KnowEm Username Search: Social Media, Domains and Trademarks," *KnowEm*, accessed July 21, 2014, http://knowem.com/.

than 12 characters if possible. **Every single one of the top 25 brands in the world are 12 characters or less**[16]. I repeat:

EVERY SINGLE ONE OF THE TOP 25 BRANDS IN THE WORLD ARE 12 CHARACTERS OR LESS.

That is assuming, of course, that you can use an abbreviated form such as "GE" instead of "General Electric."

3. Is it easy to say out loud?

No matter how clever you are at marketing, there is a very good chance that your best method for finding customers will be word of mouth. Your business name has to be easy to say in order for people to talk about you.

Amazon was originally named Cadabra. During one conversation between founder Jeff Bezos and his lawyer, the lawyer mistook the name for "Cadaver." Bezos realized that others could make the same mistake and changed it to Amazon.

---

16 Kurt Badenhausen, "The World's Most Valuable Brands," *Forbes*, last modified November 6, 2013, http://www.forbes.com/powerful-brands/.

4. Do you like it?

You will have to say it a lot, so you better like it. It will grow on you to some extent, but don't start with something you don't like.

5. Does it make sense for your idea?

As a bonus, if the name clearly makes sense for your idea, then it's a real winner.

DropBox says what it does without being too specific. Our WordPress conversions plugin is called ConvertPress[17].

6. Broader is better.

You are an early stage company, so it's hard to know exactly what you will be doing down the track. Don't use specific keywords in your domain name or specific mentions of your service or your location. This could easily change and create a bit of unnecessary work for you.

---

17 "ConvertPress - WordPress landing pages and opt in forms," *ConvertPress*, accessed August 23, 2014, http://convertpress.com/.

As a general rule, something broader will serve you better. Twitter started as a text message platform, but the name works perfectly well for the web and mobile app it is today.

A Simple Checklist for Choosing the Best Company Name

Put your ten names into this checklist and choose whichever one gets the best score.

Name	Is it taken?	Is it simple?	Sound good?	Do you like it?	Is it sensible?	Is it broad?	Score/6
Name 1							
Name 2							
Name 3							
Name 4							
Name 5							

Day 3 Task - *Come up with a bunch of potential business names and evaluate them against the criteria above. Choose whichever one makes the most sense to you and run with it. Grab the best domain you can for that name. I have this chart and other resources at wpcurve.com/7daystartup*

Day 4 - Build a Website in One Day for under $100

"A good plan, violently executed now, is better than a perfect plan next week." **General George S. Patton, Jr.**

Now that you have a business idea and name, you are ready to start articulating what your message will be. The purpose of the landing page is twofold:

1. To start communicating with customers and learning how they respond.
2. To begin to build what will ultimately sell your product.

You don't want to spend weeks or months on the landing page. One day is a reasonable amount of time to get a page ready.

There are a few general approaches you can take with setting up your site.

1. Create a site designed to capture email addresses before you ultimately launch in four days' time.

2. Create a site that "pre-sells" your product before you launch it.
3. Create the actual sales page that you'll use on launch day.

It's imperative that on Day 7 you have a page with a payment button on it, because that is the only way you'll learn if people want what you are offering.

Before then, it's useful to put up a quick landing page that communicates something small about the idea. Even if it's only for a few days, it doesn't hurt to start communicating. You might be able to build a small list to email when you launch.

I'll run through the detailed steps of how to set up a WordPress site for under $100. If you already know how to set up a WordPress site, or you already have one, feel free to skip this section. Further down in the chapter I discuss a simple marketing funnel that will be useful for you.

Depending on the technology you use, the steps may be slightly different. The prices are based on advertised deals at the time of writing.

Step 1 - Register a Domain ($4 - 5 minutes)

Once you are happy with your name, it's time to register a domain. Ideally the .com is available, but if it's not you can use another extension.

- Visit godaddy.com[18]
- Search for a domain.
- Register it.

Step 2 - Set up Hosting ($4 / month - 10 minutes)

WP Curve is hosted with WP Engine. They aren't cheap, but I take the site seriously so I want the best. For now, you can get away with something simple.

If your host supports cPanel, it will make your life a lot easier. You should be able to install WordPress with just a few clicks, so check for the availability of a one-click WordPress setup before you choose a host (more on this later).

---

18 "Domain Names | The World's Largest Domain Name Registrar - GoDaddy," *GoDaddy*, accessed July 21, 2014, http://www.godaddy.com/.

- Sign up for a shared hosting plan with GoDaddy[19]or Bluehost[20]. (*Note: I'm not suggesting these are great hosts; I'm putting them forward as affordable fast options.)*
- Ask them where you need to "repoint your nameservers" to—it will be something like ns1. bluehost.com and ns2.bluehost.com *(Note: if you have your domain with GoDaddy and you wish to host with them, you won't have to change nameservers)*.
- Log in to your GoDaddy domain management console (where you bought the domain), then look for the options to "Manage Domain" and look for "Update your nameservers."
- Replace whatever is there with the nameservers from your host.

A few notes:

- The domain will take generally 2-24 hours before it shows up on your new host, so I like to do this as soon as I register the domain. Normally it's a few hours.

---

19 "Domain Names," *GoDaddy*, http://www.godaddy.com/.

20 "The Best Web Hosting | Fast Professional Website Hosting Services," *Bluehost*, accessed July 21, 2014, http://www.bluehost.com/.

- Your new host may have a temporary page showing so you know if it's working.
- If you run into problems, your host should help you. If you are nice, they will do quite a bit for you, even if they don't cover development tasks in their scope.

Step 3 - Install WordPress ($0 - 15 minutes)

Installing WordPress is easy, no matter who you are hosting with. It's made a lot easier if your host includes a tool to help with your installation. Fantastico and Softaculous are two examples of options inside the Hosting Control panels that allow you to set up WordPress quickly.

Ask your host if they have a WordPress one-click install option. If so, follow the steps for installation.

If not, you will have to do it the old-fashioned way, which is roughly 5-10 minutes work.

Here are the steps for doing it the old-fashioned way in cPanel:

1. Log into cPanel using the details provided to you when you signed up for your hosting account.

2. Click on MySQL Database Wizard.
3. Work through the process of setting up a database and a database user—remember to copy the password you create for the user and keep it somewhere safe.
4. Give the user all permissions associated with that database. There's not a lot you can break at this stage so go for it, and if you get stuck, most hosts will point you in the right direction (especially if you explain you wanted a one-click install).
5. Visit wordpress.org[21] and download the WordPress files.
6. Open the File Manager inside cPanel, click on "public_html", and then "upload."
7. Upload the WordPress .zip file.
8. In the File Manager, select the .zip file and click "Extract" at the top.
9. Visit your domain in a browser and WordPress should recognize that it's installed and needs to be configured.
10. Walk through the process of telling WordPress what database to use and setting up users, etc.

---

21 "WordPress: Blog Tool, Publishing Platform, and CMS," *WordPress*, accessed July 21, 2014, http://wordpress.org/.

That should take a few minutes, and then you're done. You have a complete WordPress installation. Congratulations; you are now running the same website platform as The New York Times!

Step 4 - Choose a Theme or Landing Page ($69 -1 hour)

The next step is to put up a "Coming Soon" page with lead capture or a theme for your live site.

It's up to you whether you want to capture emails here or you want to put up a simple one-page website. I'll provide instructions for both.

Steps for creating a simple lead capture page

- Inside WordPress, mouse over "Plugins" on the left and click "Add new."
- Enter the keywords, "SeedProd Coming Soon," and hit "Search Plugins."
- Click "Install now" next to the plugin called "Coming Soon."
- Click "Activate Plugin" to turn it on.

- On the left, mouse over "Settings" and click "Coming Soon."
- From there you can enable the "Coming Soon" page and connect it to an email system like MailChimp, Drip, or Infusionsoft to collect email addresses.

This will set up a landing page on your new homepage that will capture emails.

Steps for creating a themed WordPress page

If you don't want to set up a temporary page, you can start putting together your full site with a WordPress theme.

WordPress gives you the ability to get world class themes very cheaply and install them in seconds. I used ElegantThemes.com[22], and they sell a range of themes for just $69. The more recent themes in particular are great, with many of them being well designed, modern, and mobile-responsive.

- Visit elegantthemes.com[23] and purchase your theme.

---

22 "WordPress Themes Loved By Over 240k Customers," *Elegant Themes, Inc*, accessed July 21, 2014, http://www.elegantthemes.com/.

23 "WordPress Themes," *Elegant Themes, Inc*, http://www.elegantthemes.com/.

- Download your theme .zip file and save it to your local computer.
- Inside WordPress, mouse over "Appearance" and click "Themes."
- Click the tab called "Install Themes."
- Click upload, select the zip file and click "Install."
- After it's installed, click "Activate" and then visit the homepage to see how it looks.

Most of the time, it will need to be configured or customized to look exactly how you imagined it would. Don't get too tricky with it; just set it up the way it's designed. You can get fancier later on.

A Suggested Basic Marketing Funnel

Since you've already begun your marketing, it's useful to think about how you will be signing up customers.

I'll go into detail about how you will market your business in Day 5. For now, though, I'll suggest a basic marketing funnel as a starting point.

A marketing funnel is the process by which someone will become a customer. One that works well in a lot of cases is:

- Customer visits your website and "opts in" by handing over their email address in return for a freebie that helps solve a problem they have.
- Over time you send them useful information about that problem.
- When they are ready to buy, they visit your payment page and purchase.

For this to work, you really only need three things:

1. A page that collects email addresses. As mentioned above, "Coming Soon" can do this for a launch page. Or you can use an opt in plugin like our plugin ConvertPress.com[24] for other parts of the site.

---

24 "ConvertPress - WordPress landing pages and opt in forms," *ConvertPress*, http://convertpress.com/.

2. A system you can use to email people. I use Infusionsoft.com[25], but MailChimp.com[26] is a great free solution for a new business and getdrip.com[27] is a good lightweight automation option.
3. A page where you can sell your product/service.

This is the basic funnel my team uses across all of our businesses, so it can work for a new business idea all the way through to an established company.

I've covered the steps for setting up the email opt-in above, so now I'll look at the steps for creating your payment page.

PayPal is still by far the easiest way to get online payments happening quickly.

---

25 "Small Business CRM | Marketing Software Small Business," *Infusionsoft*, accessed July 21, 2014, http://www.infusionsoft.com/.

26 "Send Better Email," *MailChimp*, accessed July 21, 2014, http://mailchimp.com/.

27 "A Double Digit Jump in Your Conversion Rate," *The Numa Group*, accessed July 21, 2014, https://www.getdrip.com/.

- Visit paypal.com[28] and create an account if you don't have one. A personal account is generally fine as a starting point.
- Search their help for creating "Buy Now" buttons. The specific steps change regularly, but at the time of writing it's just a matter of clicking on your profile at the top and then clicking on "Selling Tools."
- Create a "Buy Now" button for one-off sales or a "Subscription" button for monthly subscriptions.
- Back on your website inside WordPress, mouse over "Pages" and click "Add Page." Enter the sales copy and images for your page, and in the "Code" view for the page, paste in the HTML script that PayPal gave you for the button.
- Save the page, then click "View Page" and give it a test. Click the payment button and make sure it takes you off to PayPal and doesn't give you an error.

Note: there is a plugin called Post Snippets[29] you can use for the PayPal code if it's giving you errors. Sometimes

---

28 "Send Money, Pay Online or Set Up a Merchant Account," *PayPal*, accessed July 21, 2014, https://www.paypal.com/home/.

29 "Post Snippets," *WordPress*, Last modified April 17, 2014, http://wordpress.org/plugins/post-snippets/.

WordPress will mess up code you place directly in the editor.

There are a few more things that will help you out enormously with your site, particularly when it comes to increasing sales and increasing opt ins.

1. The copy is extremely important and it can make or break your business. If you are just getting started with copywriting, you should use Dane Maxwell's CopyWriting Checklist[30] as a starting point.
2. When you are selling online, images make a huge difference. A professionally-designed theme is a great place to start, and the images you add in will also have a big impact.
3. Set up Google Analytics so you can understand how people are using the site. Visit google.com/analytics[31] and create an account, then install the YOAST Google Analytics plugin in WordPress to hook it up.

---

30 Dane Maxwell, "The Copywriting Checklist: How To Sell The Crap Out Of Great Products & Services," *Mixergy*, accessed July 21, 2014, http://mixergy.com/Master-Class/Copywriting/TheCopywritingChecklist.pdf.

31 "Google Analytics Official Website," *Google*, accessed July 21, 2014, http://www.google.com/analytics/.

Set up conversion goals for your purchase or your email opt-in.

Ready to go!

The power of WordPress is that you have the ability to customize and expand your site.

The site you build on Day 4 is a good place to start, but the important thing is that you've built it on a platform with virtually no limits. You are using the same platform as CNN, The New York Times, and Forbes. On top of that, there are easy ways to improve your site and get access to support if you need it. You have the world's best content marketing platform at your fingertips.

As you get more ideas, add them to your site and start paying attention to what feedback you get. You can also keep an eye on analytics and, ideally, what conversions you are getting on that landing page.

Day 4 Task *- Build yourself a website! If you need help setting things up, check out wpcurve.com/7daystartup for many of the worksheets and exercises.*

Day 5 - 10 Ways to Market Your Business

This is definitely a stumbling block for many people when starting their business. It's fine to open your doors, but how do you get in front of the right people? I don't want this to hold you back, so I've provided 10 specific stories about how other companies gained early customers. You will find many more up at *wpcurve.com/7daystartup*.

It's up to you whether you do these on Day 7 when you launch, the days following, or even now. I'd suggest you don't plan past the first 30 days. Give yourself enough activities in that first month of business to try a bunch of strategies. Figure out what works for you and what doesn't. Make sure you get your product in front of enough qualified buyers. This will help you learn what works for you and what to do next.

If you want to get a copy of this plan so you can start crafting your own as you read this chapter, you can grab the Google doc from wpcurve.com/7daystartup.

The main purpose of marketing is to get your product in front of qualified buyers. This means getting people to your landing page or your sales page. A lot of these suggestions are online strategies for generating traffic to your site. However, you might find face-to-face strategies work better for you, so I've included a few of those as well.

Also remember that these ideas are all designed to market your business quickly. There are many other powerful ways you can market new products. Partnerships with other companies can be extremely fruitful, but they don't generally come together quickly. Crowdfunding sites can also be great ways to launch physical products, but it's difficult to get backers quickly. The following ideas can all be done in the first few days after launching and can result in real paying customers right away.

1 - Create Content on Your Site

Most of our early customers came as a result of our content marketing efforts.

Before I give you my own notes, here's how Liam from Trak.io[32] used the same technique to sign up 217 paid customers in the first few months of launching.

Liam researched some rising trends and realized that at the time "Growth Hacking" was a popular term. He looked at what was out there and saw that most of the content was discussing what the job role meant. There wasn't a whole lot of implement-worthy info that startup founders and marketers could lift from the page and apply to their business.

Liam jumped on this opportunity and published a few very detailed blog posts on the topic. He gained around 2,500 free signups through this tactic after a few posts did particularly well.

Liam's business is now growing organically, but this was just the boost he needed. It enabled him to get enough early customers to start building a great product with direct customer feedback.

---

32 "Affordable Customer Success For SaaS Companies," *Trak.io*, accessed July 21, 2014, http://trak.io/.

I agree with Liam when he says content marketing isn't the fastest way to get customers. But he also agrees that it's cheap, it's fun, and it helps other people. That's a lot of good reasons to consider using content in your business. On top of that, there are some things you can do to get quicker results like publishing your content on other high trafficked sites.

Here are a few quick notes from my own experience:

1. Create in-depth content based around the customer problems that your business solves.
2. Make content as actionable and useful to your target audience as possible.
3. It can't be boring. Don't just create content around your area of expertise. Create anything that is interesting to your potential customers.
4. Optimize your site for email opt-ins so you can get people back to your site by sending emails.
5. Don't worry about SEO. Focus predominantly on creating useful content.
6. Try a bunch of content mediums and look for where you get traction (on-site written content, infographics, videos, podcasts, ebooks or whitepapers, etc.).

The key is to make sure you know what sort of content produces the outcomes you want. If you don't have a big audience, then creating lots of content on your own site won't generate lots of short-term sales, but it will build long-term momentum. In the early days, do more off-site work like podcast interviews and guest posts to put yourself in front of new audiences.

I'm extremely passionate about content marketing and I've put a lot of free resources up at *wpcurve.com/7daystartup* for you to check out.

2 - Start Sending Emails

Your email list will become one of the most valuable assets in your business. A list of people who trust you, that you can contact exclusively whenever you like, is a gold mine. It can take time to build up a decent list, but the best thing you can do is start as early as possible. I suggest building an email list before you launch and continually looking at ways of growing your list.

WP Curve's email list is around 12,000 people. Here are the top ways the company has gone about building the list:

1. Adding people I knew early on. Well-known Tech Blogger Andrew Chen did the same thing. He started writing emails to his friends at first. This got him in the habit of sending the emails, and before long he had a big list to talk to.
2. Set up landing pages that you can point people to. One of the highest-converting landing pages will be the page you have before you launch. This can become your email list after you launch.
3. Make sure you are sending out a lot of high quality, relevant information. Don't try to sell to everyone on the list.
4. Give away something relevant and valuable to people to get them onto the list. I have had good results with free software, plugins, templates, ebooks, and training courses. This book itself was given away free in return for an (optional) email address.
5. Create great content on your site and provide giveaways (lead magnets) that are related to that content. For example, I gave away a Conversion Review Template on any of my content that talks about conversions.
6. Keep all of your emails personal and encourage people to reply to the emails. This can be a great way to learn what customers want and gain lightning-fast

feedback on your business ideas. On top of that, you get opportunities to help people out and build up some goodwill among your online community. People will help you if you help them first.

The easiest way to get started with email marketing is signing up for a free account on MailChimp.com[33]. I used MailChimp for years before migrating to Infusionsoft.com[34] for some more advanced features.

If you want to access the template that helps you increase your email conversions, you can grab it for free at wpcurve.com/7daystartup.

3 - Podcasting

When I sold my last agency I went on a mission to create as much content as I could. One of the best things I did was start a podcast. Not so much for the immediate lead generation, but more for the ongoing networking opportunities.

---

33 "Send Better Email," *MailChimp*, http://mailchimp.com/.

34 "Small Business CRM," *Infusionsoft*, http://www.infusionsoft.com/.

My podcast, Startup Chat, is only moderately popular. But it has been the easiest way I can imagine to network with some amazing entrepreneurs.

We've built real relationships with influencers in our space including Neil Patel, Sean Ellis, James Schramko, Noah Kagan, and Dan Andrews.

Everyone I know who has started a podcast lists the networking as the number one benefit. If you are like me, and you don't love the idea of calling an influencer just to talk, then a podcast interview is an awesome alternative. You are creating free content for them and helping to spread their message, so you don't feel bad asking for the interview.

Some other benefits of podcasting:

1. It's quite easy to do. Not everyone can write, but most people can talk.
2. Hearing your voice builds people's trust significantly.
3. It opens you up to entire new marketing channels like iTunes and Stitcher Radio.
4. It allows you to have one-on-one time with people in entirely new situations (when they are driving, at the gym etc.).

5. It gives you great authority in your field. A lot of people have a blog, but podcasting is still fairly new. I think people assume it's difficult and you have to have a studio to do it, but that's not the case. Most podcasters I know, even the ones with seven-figure businesses, are doing their podcast from home.

I'm also a big advocate of going on other people's podcasts. When you have your own podcast, you'll start getting invitations to appear on other ones. It takes hardly any time and they do all the work, so jump on it! I'm not above asking people if I can come on their podcast either. It builds an association between you and another influencer, it's fun, easy, and spreads your message to new audiences.

If you are interested in getting started with podcasting, I have prepared a detailed guide which you can get for free at wpcurve.com/7daystartup.

4 - Forums and Online Groups

Online forums or social media groups can be a great place to build networks and find customers.

When Damian Thompson wanted to launch his new business, Linchpin.net[35], he started with a private forum of entrepreneurs called dynamitecircle.com[36]. Damian was a trusted member of the group, having been one of the original members. When he posted an offer, a number of people took him up on it straight away.

Damian signed up his first four monthly customers for his marketing automation service from that forum. This gave him $3,000 / month of recurring revenue, which was enough to make his first hire. And guess where that staff member came from? Yep, from the forum, too! 18 months on, Damien has built his business up to $30,000 / month.

Forums have a certain level of trust built in, so a lot of the hard work is done if you are already a valued member. I signed up my first customer for WP Curve in the same forum—and Damian was that customer!

Social media groups can offer similar results.

---

35 "Demand Generation Done for You," *Linchpin*, accessed July 21, 2014, http://linchpin.net/.

36 "DynamiteCircle," *DynamiteCircle*, accessed July 21, 2014, http://www.dynamitecircle.com/.

One of the benefits of groups like these is that they are paid groups, which pre-qualifies the members. The fact that they are willing and able to pay to be in the group makes them, in turn, far more likely to pay you.

If you are a member of groups like this then they could be a good place to start your marketing. Be conscious of the rules and don't oversell. Even just offering a deal or a freebie to members of the group might be enough to kickstart some business with real customers. If you aren't a member of a paid group in your niche, I'd definitely consider joining one.

5 - Guest Blogging

I've talked about content marketing already, but I feel guest blogging deserves its own section due to its ability to drive leads quickly.

When Terry Lin worked in finance, there were a few niche gossip blogs that folks in the industry would follow. Not the big players like Forbes, Wall Street Journal, etc., but smaller ones with content revolving around bonuses, employment, and a lifestyle relevant to the banker in major cities like NYC, London, Tokyo, Hong Kong, and Singapore.

When Terry left the industry to start his men's accessories business, ballerleather.com[37], he approached the editor of one of these blogs for a guest post. He planned on sharing his story of starting a business and the lessons he's learned since leaving the industry. It was a unique angle and the content was different than most of the usual topics. From initial outreach to the post going live, it was done within a week.

The article was only a short 600-word piece, but it was highly relevant to folks in the finance industry. Terry's bio at the bottom included a link to his business, and by the end of the day he had made $700 in sales.

The key for Terry was just being honest and upfront while constructing a genuinely real and interesting post to share with his audience. The other crucial factor is that he knew his ideal customers extremely well. Effective guest blogging is like every other form of marketing: it's all about targeting. If you can get your message in front of the right people, it will work well. If you get the message in front of irrelevant people, it won't work at all.

37 Terry Lin, "BALLER Leather Goods Co.," *Baller*, accessed July 21, 2014, http://ballerleather.com/.

6 - Listing Sites

Prateek Dayal created a help desk system called SupportBee.com[38]. When he launched, he visited a number of app comparison sites and added Support Bee in where he could.

After adding his app to alternativeto.net[39], people would find the software after researching alternatives to other help desk tools. He started getting a few free signups a day and has had many more paying customers come from the free listing.

In every industry there are a range of sites that list businesses in different ways. Some examples could be:

- If you were a web designer, you could submit your nice designs to CSS directories.

---

38 Prateek Dayal, "The Easiest Way to Manage Customer Support Emails," *SupportBee*, accessed July 21, 2014, https://supportbee.com/.

39 "Social Software Recommendations," *AlternativeTo*, Accessed July 21, 2014, http://alternativeto.net/.

- If you are a startup, you could submit your idea to startup sites like Betali.st[40] and KillerStartups.com[41].
- Any kind of product or service with a nice landing page I would submit to producthunt.com[42], a booming product listing site.
- If you created an app, you could submit it to Appvita.com[43] or Cloudli.st[44].
- If you have some kind of certified skill, there might be a central site that lists people with your skill or qualification.
- If you have a software app that integrates with other apps, you can apply to be in their integration directory. This is often cited by software product owners as a great way to get in front of qualified

40 "Discover and get early access to tomorrow's startups," *Beta List*, accessed July 21, 2014, http://betalist.com/.

41 "Where Internet Entrepreneurs Are The Stars!" *KillerStartups*, accessed July 21, 2014, http://www.killerstartups.com/.

42 "Product Hunt," *Product Hunt*, accessed July 21, 2014, http://www.producthunt.com/.

43 "Discovering web-based applications that just make life better," *AppVita*, accessed July 21, 2014, http://www.appvita.com/.

44 "The cloud's list," *Cloudlist*, Accessed July 21, 2014, http://www.cloudli.st/.

> buyers, and I also used this to get a handful of paying customers early on with Informly.

Usually, Googling will reveal a whole bunch of potential sites in any industry. You'd be amazed at the amount of traffic some of these sites get. If you can get some good traction, you will get a lot of visitors and maybe some email opt-ins or customers.

7 - Webinars

John Dumas started daily podcasting at entrepreneuronfire.com[45] in September 2012. I spoke with him in December after he'd recorded 115 episodes with entrepreneurs. At that stage he was getting 100,000 monthly downloads but he wasn't making much money. In the 18 month since then, John has made over 1.3 million dollars.

Most of his revenue comes by selling memberships to his online training community for podcasters called Podcasters Paradise. In his most recent monthly report (June 2014) he

45 John Dumas, "Entrepreneur On Fire Business Podcast," *Entrepreneur On Fire*, accessed July 21, 2014, http://www.entrepreneuronfire.com/.

attributed $134,000 in revenue to membership sales, 86% of which came directly from webinars.

This is John's exact process:

- He built up a large audience. Obviously this took him some time but the same could be done quickly on a much smaller scale.
- He gives away freebies on his site like ebooks in return for an email address. After you enter your email address you are taken to a page that talks about a free webinar on podcasting.
- The webinars provide a lot of value and help people get started with podcasting. For people who are interested in more information he has a special deal for membership to the community.
- John routinely gets hundreds of people onto these weekly webinars and closes thousands in sales.

You can learn John's exact process at webinaronfire.com[46].

46 John Dumas, "Webinar On Fire," *Entrepreneur On Fire*, accessed July 21, 2014, http://www. entrepreneuronfire.com/.

If you think a webinar could be the right fit for you and your audience, give it a go. Make sure you record it and the worst case is it ends up being a useful video to post on your site.

8 - Presenting

Organizing local, in-person events has been a winning strategy for all types of businesses for a long time; from local small businesses to global software companies like Hubspot, Constant Contact, and Salesforce.

Adam Franklin uses local workshops, meetups, and conferences to help attendees with their web marketing. In turn this helps position his web marketing firm, BluewireMedia.com[47], as a leader. While other firms were obsessing over SEO tactics and Adwords, Adam and his team were putting on live events.

The events were profitable exercises on their own, but they also brought in countless leads and high-value clients to

47 "Strategic Advertising and Marketing Solutions," *Bluewire Media*, accessed July 21, 2014, http://bluewiremedia.com/.

his business. On the feedback forms, some attendees would literally write "we want to engage your services" and become clients the next day.

It also elevated Adam's authority level to a point where, in a few short years, he became a traditionally-published author of the book *Web Marketing That Works* and a well-known social media speaker.

Doing live, local events is a powerful form of content marketing. The only difference from other methods is it's done in person, which helps strengthen ties and cement business relationships faster. Events can be daunting to host, because what happens if no one shows up? But they can pay off handsomely if you are game to try.

If this is a skill area for you, don't hesitate to put on an event and use it as a way to generate leads.

9 - Doing Free Work

There are so many variations of doing free work, and I love them all!

Derek Murphy had been a book editor for a few years and he started doing book covers for his own books. He then offered them for free to other authors. In fact, Derek did this book's cover design after he reached out and offered to do it for free.

He was able to get a bunch of testimonials and referrals from some high-profile indie publishing authors and bloggers as a result of the free covers.

He has designed book covers for hundreds of authors and is the recommended provider of book covers for a number of other high-profile bloggers.

When Clint Mayer started out with his online marketing consultancy oracledigital.com.au[48] in 2010, he decided to do SEO video audits for free. He would either offer them to people who asked for advice or he'd do them cold and send them to people who were spending up big on Yellow Pages.

---

48 Clint Mayer, "SEO, Google Adwords, Data Analysis, Content Strategies, & CRO in Perth," *Oracle Digital*, accessed July 21, 2014, http://www.oracledigital.com.au/.

Those efforts produced a number of paid customers, including one who has paid $150k over that four-year period.

I love this strategy of marketing a business and I get behind it every time I see it in action. Towards the end of last year, someone handed me a loaf of bread in a parking lot. Seemed legit. They said it was from a bakery opening around the corner and I'd love it.

I did love it, and I posted it on Instagram and Facebook and anywhere else I could. Within weeks most of the people I knew from my local area knew about this bakery. It's now one of the most popular bakeries/cafes in the area.

Early on your main challenge will be getting people to use your product or service. If you can do that then you'll start learning a lot about what you need to do to perfect it. You'll also gather testimonials and referrals which will help drive future growth.

Note this is to help spread the word, it's not a validation exercise. Free users are not the same as paying customers.

10 - Media Coverage

Getting press attention for your company can be a huge bonus. If it's well targeted, it leads to direct customers. Perhaps a bigger benefit is the extra proof and credibility you get as a result.

WP Curve has been featured by WP Engine, ShoeString startups, LifeHacker, Forbes, inc.com, and Fox News. My team got a lot out of those mentions including direct signups, logos for our homepage, a lot of social media activity, and attention from others in the industry.

I didn't have the money to pay a PR agency, so my team and I had to tackle it ourselves. Here are some of the things the team has done to get press coverage:

1. Pulled lists of relevant journalists to contact about running stories.
2. Chased our entrepreneurial friends, who had been featured and looked for intros to the journalist who covered them.
3. Paid attention to parts of our business that could be newsworthy and looked for stories. For example, I'd spent 12 months building a business that was losing

money and then within 23 days had made WP Curve profitable. I pitched this idea to Startup Daily, who published an article about the story[49].

4. Dropped everything for opportunities to be featured in the media. When Clayton Morris mentioned to Alex that he could potentially chat to him about Wordpress, he jumped to action. Alex booked flights to New York, crammed a TV presenters' course in, bought a new jacket (for $700, mind you), and a week later he was on Fox TV[50].
5. Talked about ourselves a lot. It's uncomfortable at times, particularly when putting all of our revenue numbers up on our blog[51]. But this gets people talking and interesting stories emerge.
6. Sent some of our best articles to other websites, to help with those relationships.

---

49 Tasnuva Bindi, "Tech startup becomes profitable in 23 days," *Startup Daily*, last modified July 31, 2013, http://www.startupdaily.com.au/2013/07/tech-startup-becomes-profitable-in-23-days-31072013/.

50 Alex McClafferty, interviewed by Clayton Morris, "WPCurve takes WordPress to the next level," *Fox News* video, 6:25, March 21, 2014, http://video.foxnews.com/v/3372912504001/wpcurve-takes-wordpress-to-the-next-level/.

51 "Monthly report Archives," *WPCurve*, accessed July 21, 2014, http://wpcurve.com/category/monthly-report-2/.

I've stayed away from crazy marketing stunts, but no doubt that can be effective as well. In the end they are looking for a story—journalists don't want to feature you for the sake of it. Look for stories in everything you are doing and maintain good relationships with journalists and influencers.

This does take time, but if you can promote unique stories around your launch, that tends to be a good time to be featured.

This chapter could have been 50 Ways to Market Your Business

This chapter was originally going to be "50 Ways to Market Your Business." What I realized while writing, though, was that most of these methods were the same thing. Marketing is really just about getting your message out to qualified people as efficiently as possible. Connect your message with them as best you can.

You might do it by getting noticed through a unique service offering or a giveaway.

You might do it by paid advertising.

You might do it by throwing a party.

What matters is that you do it in the way that utilizes your unique strengths and gets you customers! For some people, that's face to face networking; for others, it's creating content. Test out a bunch of options and double down on what is working well. Look for sources of momentum and do more of what is working.

Day 5 Task - *Build a list of what marketing methods you are going to choose. Put together a rough plan for the first week or two of your launch. To make it easier, I've created a template for you to use at wpcurve.com/7daystartup.*

Day 6 - Set Targets

The point of launching a business quickly is that you can get real data from real customers. This will help you determine if the business is having an impact. But how do you know what a good result is?

In examples where companies really take off, you don't need to worry about this step. Companies like Buffer and Dropbox never had to worry about whether or not they were onto something; thousands of people were signing up. It was obvious!

Similarly, when companies are an outright flop, that tends to be obvious as well.

They are the one-percenters. Most companies fall in the middle, so it's important to have some sort of framework around whether or not your business is going well.

The way I like to think about this is to focus on the One Metric That Matters (OMTM) at different stages in your business, a concept I got from *Lean Analytics*.

When you launch, it makes sense to focus on the number of people who sign up and pay you. Set a reasonable target that takes into consideration your reach and your marketing efforts and price point.

People have a tendency to set really aggressive targets in business and I've found those to be potentially de-motivating. Most businesses will naturally grow over time if the fundamentals are right. When you are starting out, you have a big hurdle to get over. Most people want a few runs on the board before they put their trust in a business. Shoot for a few customers early on and set a realistic monthly growth rate from there.

For WP Curve, I wanted to get ten customers in the first month or around $500 in MRR. From there I wanted to grow at 10% per month for at least the first six months. This was bare minimum and thankfully WP Curve outpaced this significantly.

With any business I've started, my primary goal has been to get to a point where I'm paying myself a reasonable wage as early as possible. The figure I've always used is $40,000 per year. If I can get to the point where I'm paying myself a wage of $40,000, I know I have enough there to keep the business going. Eventually I have the faith that I'll continue to improve this number.

With WP Curve, I got ten customers in the first week. It broke even after 23 days and I hit my $40k annual estimated wage in about six months, as a result of exceeding 10% growth each month. After 13 months that amount was over $130,000.

The metric of choice has always been MRR. I've kept a spreadsheet from day one that translates this number into an estimated wage for each founder and reports monthly growth rates.

Every business is different and your OMTM may be different. Recurring businesses are easier to understand. Your OMTM is getting more people signing up than those leaving. On the other hand, product businesses or project based businesses are a bit trickier.

Here are some general principles around setting your OMTM target:

- Make it a financial metric, not a vanity metric like website visits or Facebook likes.

- Pay particular attention to who is signing up. If it's just your friends, then that's very different from the general public.

SAVE YOUR EXCITEMENT UNTIL YOU LAND PEOPLE YOU DON'T KNOW AS CUSTOMERS.

- Set a goal for the first month and re-visit it each month after that. My team uses a live Google doc for tracking financials. It requires manual updating, but it's great for motivation and it allows you to have live estimates instead of relying on old data in accounting systems. There's a free template at wpcurve.com/7daystartup.
- Don't measure something that no longer represents an important metric for your business. The OMTM will change over time.

Below are two tables. First is a table providing you examples of what your OMTM could be at any given time. Next you will see an example of a live financial metrics spreadsheet for a typical business.

Stage	What to measure	How to measure it	What represents success
Problem/Idea Validation	Do people need this product?	Ask your current customers how disappointed they would be if you closed down the service.	If 40% say they would be disappointed or very disappointed, you are probably onto something.
MVP Launch	How many people have signed up for it?	Total signups in the first week or month.	It's up to you. I wanted to see at least ten monthly recurring customers within the first month.
Business Model Validation	Profit margin	The percentage profit you will make with the founders working in the business. The percentage profit you will make if you had to hire replacements for the founders.	Ideally there is enough profit margin for the business to hypothetically run and grow without the founders. Percentages will vary significantly based on a lot of factors. In my recurring services business, I aim for around 50%.
Growth	CPA and LTV	Use the CPA Calculator at wpcurve.com/7daystartup to work out how much customers cost to acquire. LTV: A simple Churn measure is the number of subscribers lost during the period divided by the total subscribers at the start of the period.	Ideally LTV should be a lot higher than CPA. It can take a while to get to that point.

OMTM gauge[52]

Live financial metrics

	B	C	D	E	F	G	H
2	**Key numbers**						
3							
4							
5	Current MRR	$13,999					
6	Cost per customer	$29					
7	Fixed costs	$6,061					
8	Current clients	206					
9	Monthly growth target	10%					
10							
11		**Founder Profit**	**MRR**	**Annual runrate**	**Costs**	**Total subscriptions**	**MRR Growth**
12	May 2013	-$3,846	$476	$5,712	$1,117	16	
13	June 2013	-$1,259	$907	$10,886	$1,117	27	91%
14	July 2013	$2,574	$1,546	$18,552	$1,117	39	70%
15	Aug 2013	$7,956	$2,668	$32,016	$1,342	52	73%
16	Sep 2013	$8,958	$3.293	$39,516	$1,800	64	23%
17	Oct 2013	$19,563	$6,196	$74,350	$2,937	123	88%
18	Nov 2013	$31,920	$8,371	$100,452	$3,051	155	36%
19	Dec 2013	$36,306	$9,812	$117,744	$3,761	178	17%
20	Jan 2014	$40,626	$11,310	$135,720	$4,539	201	15%
21	Feb 2014	$42,918	$11,868	$142,416	$4,715	202	5%
22	Mar 2014	$49,428	$13,604	$163,248	$5,366	206	15%
23	Apr 2014	$47,626	$13,999	$167,988	$6,061	210	3%
24	May 2014	$53,068	$15,399	$184,787	$6,551	227	10%
25	Jun 2014	$58,316	$16,939	$203,268	$7,219	240	10%
26	Jul 2014	$64,068	$18,633	$223,592	$7,955	274	10%
27	Aug 2014	$70,384	$20,496	$245,951	$8,764	302	10%
28	September 2014	$77,353	$22,546	$270,546	$9,653	332	10%
29	October 2014	$85,009	$24,800	$297,601	$10,632	365	10%
30	November 2014	$93,429	$27,280	$327,361	$11,709	401	10%
31	December 2014	$102,692	$30,008	$360,097	$12,893	442	10%

Example of a live financial metrics spreadsheet

The truth is that running a business is never black and white. How do you know when you are onto something or when you should give up? This is one of the most common questions I get asked. Unfortunately I can never really answer. You need to use your own judgment to determine if you feel like you are onto something that will meet your expectations.

---

52 40%, from Sean Ellis, http://www.startup-marketing.com/the-startup-pyramid/

Focus on what your paying customers are saying and how many people continue to pay you, and you can't go too far wrong.

Day 6 Task - *Create a spreadsheet that covers the first few months in business, the number of signups, revenue, estimated costs, and monthly growth. You can use the template provided at wpcurve.com/7daystartup to get started.*

Day 7 - Launch

"If you are not embarrassed by the first version of your product, you've launched too late."
Reid Hoffman

Launch day is like every other day. It is an important day, because you enter into the period of real data collection and running a real business with paying customers.

But it's just a day.

Here is a short list of ideas to get you started:

- Put up your live website with the payment button. Include as many options as you can for people to contact you. You want to talk to customers and potential customers as much as possible from today onwards. Consider having live chat, email, physical address, phone number, and social media profiles.[53]

53 I have another business www.helloify.com, that is a great option for live chat software.

- Email anyone who is on your pre-launch list. Thank them for their interest and ask them to sign up if your offering is suitable for them.
- Post an update to social networks and any forums or groups that allow you to do so.
- If you are a member of any forums that allow you to have a signature that mentions your business, update those signatures with a specific call to action.
- Tell your friends and press contacts and ask them to share the news.
- Thank people who have helped you get to launch day.
- Continue with your influencer outreach. Launch day might be too soon to ask for a favor, but it doesn't hurt to mention it.
- Publish a post on your blog about the launch. Thank the people who have helped you, and include a call to action for people to purchase.
- Ask your entrepreneurial friends to share the news. If you help people out 90% of the time and only ask for help 10% of the time, the launch day is a good day to ask for help.
- Go back over your marketing plan and start executing each of the items you wrote down. Podcast interviews are a good one to do on launch day; it gets

you talking to people and keeps the buzz going. Start tracking which methods are working well for you.

- I'd love to know if you've launched a business using this method, so give me a shout out on social media @thedannorris or #7daystartup. I'll even help spread the word if I think my audience would be interested.

The most important thing is... don't stress! A launch will very rarely make or break a successful sustainable business, which is what you are trying to build.

Dan Andrews of Tropical MBA[54] has said that it takes 1,000 days to build a business.

Launch day is just 1 out of 1,000.

***Day 7 Task** - Launch and start executing your marketing plan.*

54 Dan Andrews, "The 1000 Day Rule: What Living the Dream Really Looks Like," *TMBA*, last modified September 8, 2011, http://www.tropicalmba.com/living-the-dream/.

REFINE YOUR BUSINESS MODEL

"Growth is never by mere chance; it is the result of forces working together."
James Cash Penney

Great work; you've launched! The planning and launch are done. But the real work happens now. Now you have to hustle up real paying customers; you have to pay attention to whether they are paying, whether they are staying, and whether they are referring. And you have to listen to what they say, to work out if and how you are going to grow this business.

On top of that, you need to build the business into something that is fundamentally profitable or else it will never grow, so I want to spend a bit of time on that.

Creating a product and getting customers is great, but businesses will not survive and thrive without growing profits over time. Having a good idea and paying customers on launch day doesn't guarantee that will happen.

For you to achieve ongoing growth, you need a self-sufficient business model.

The reason this chapter comes *after* launch is because your business model will mostly be dictated by your customers. For example, we've started recurring businesses before, only to change them later because customers just wouldn't accept a recurring fee for that particular product. Once you figure these sorts of things out, you can work out a way to grow the business.

I don't want to talk down the importance of getting your first few customers, because that in itself is hard. You can't stop there. Some businesses are fundamentally unscalable and some are built with growth already in their DNA.

Building a Business That Couldn't Grow

I've mentioned that my previous agency was simply unable to grow profitably. You'd be surprised how many businesses are designed in this way. The model is fundamentally wrong, and makes them impossible to grow. The numbers just don't add up.

Let's think about what I would have had to do to grow my previous agency.

1. For starters, I would have had to get more leads. Since leads came through face-to-face meetings and content, that would mean hiring a salesperson and a content creator. Those two hires alone would have completely killed any profit there was in the business. This wasn't an option at any stage of the business; I simply couldn't afford to make the hire.
2. I could have increased the costs of my projects. That would have helped short-term profits. However, high-cost, low-quantity sales are difficult to scale. They would have turned the business into a higher-touch sales machine and I would have needed salespeople. I know other similar business owners

who tried and failed as this is a huge risk. It was an extremely competitive field, too, so higher costs would have probably meant lower sales.

3. I wasn't capable of managing any more clients, so I would have had to hire staff to replace me. Clients had been trained to receive individual local service, so I would have needed a local client manager. I did this at one point and, of course, it killed my margins and was unsustainable.
4. I would have had to physically get through more work. The work was complex. We had writers, coders, designers, project managers, and SEOs. I myself did a lot of jobs including conversion optimization, copywriting, etc. Some of that can be done with affordable contractors; some can't. The work's complexity would require more project managers, which also would have been difficult to do with affordable contractors. Again, it would mean more expensive local staff. All of these costs would have completely killed the profits.

The thing is, none of this occurred to me when I was quoting a website for $2,000. That seemed like a lot. And it was enough to get me to a certain point, but it was doomed to fail.

I tried everything you can think of, but I couldn't grow the business profitably. When revenues went up so did the costs and stress, but profits remained stagnant.

In order to grow it, I had to scrap it and start over again.

Every decision you make about how you design your business and what work to take on will impact its ability to grow.

Build a Business With Growth in its DNA

I did a lot of soul searching after I sold that business. I knew I did a lot wrong, and I wanted to make sure I didn't make the same mistakes next time.

I also want to make sure you don't make the same mistakes, so I've come up with five criteria for building a business with growth in its DNA.

1. Profit Margin

It's easy to work out whether or not your business has profit margin, or to at least estimate it early on.

Imagine not being involved in your business at all—everything the customer experiences gets handled by a team of people or systems. How much does it cost you to keep that customer and how much revenue do they generate?

The actual, acceptable percentage will depend on a lot of things, but obviously you have to be making more than it's costing you to service each customer. For our services startup

I decided a reasonable figure was double. That is: half of our revenue is costs, half is profit, so I'd have a 50% margin. If it costs $50 / month to service a customer, I would price the service at $100.

This is a very rough rule but I've found when you be truly honest about your real costs, most small businesses don't have a margin this high.

I solved this problem by cutting out 99% of what I offered and only offering a service that I knew affordable contractors could excel at it. This enabled me to have an acceptable margin in the business of around 50%.

For you, it could mean something different—perhaps just charging more. However I would warn you about falling into the trap of charging more. It's much like cutting costs, you can only do it till a point. I much prefer having a reasonable margin and getting more customers at that price. If you are in a big market, that will be a never ending growth strategy.

2. Large Market

I'm not into niches. I want to make sure whatever I start could be a $1,000,000 business in a few years, ideally more. I hope you are the same.

If you want something that grows, it has to have something to grow *into*, and the last thing you want is to kill your momentum by hitting a ceiling. I've mentioned serving a large market previously, but since it's such a big growth inhibitor, it bears repeating here.

This is part of your business model as it's a decision about who you say "yes" or "no" to. Make sure there is enough potential in what you are doing to have a continually-growing business.

3. Asset Building

When I sold my business, I learned that project clients were worth very little. The website and the recurring clients were transferable assets. The historical revenue from project work wasn't worth much at all.

When you sign up additional customers, are you building an asset? What other assets are growing naturally as you work on your business? Assets help your business grow and make it worth something when you sell.

A business is like a house. You can never imagine yourself leaving, but you do. Every single time.

Any type of intellectual property is a great example, but not every business can have that.

WHAT ARE YOU WORKING ON TODAY THAT WILL MAKE YOU INDESTRUCTIBLE TOMORROW?

4. Simple Business Model

Having a simple product and a simple value proposition makes everything else easier. From elevator pitches to growth tracking to hiring—the more complex a model, the harder it is to know when things are going well. If you can't measure it, you can't manage it.

A business with one basic product like Buffer or Dropbox is a growth machine. If you want a scalable business model, it's much better to work on one simple offering than thirty different ones. Keep this in mind as you focus your attention and don't get distracted. Follow the momentum.

5. Recurring or Predictable Revenue

Having a simple MRR model makes everything easier. There are other benefits like predictable revenue, simple metrics, simple goals, easy-to-see growth/growth sources, easy resourcing/scaling, and constant sources of motivation. A year in and I am still manually updating the MRR on a daily basis and giving my team members virtual high-fives.

Quite often, in a recurring monthly business, a bad month is just growing less than every other month. There isn't a huge roller coaster of good months and bad months like you have in other businesses. Increasing the amount of money you are going to make next month and every month after is a great feeling. A simple MRR model has an inherent growth trait. The equation is simple: Have more customers signing up than leaving, and you will grow.

Not every service suits a recurring model, so you could think about other ways to build predictable revenue. Seriously consider offering a recurring aspect to your business if you think there's a chance you can make it work. It will often mean fewer customers, but if those customers are one-off sales that don't contribute to long term growth, then you might be better off without them. If your testing shows it can't work and you are leaving too much business on the table, then focus on making sure your revenue is predictable.

To help, I'll give you some examples of business models and how they fit the criteria.

Criteria	Profit margin	Large market	Asset	Simple	Recurring	Best practice example
SaaS (Software as a Service)	Yes, extremely high margins	Yes, except for niche SaaS	Yes; look at some of the valuations!	Yes	Yes	dropbox.com
Service as a service	Yes, margins aren't as good as SaaS though	Yes, as long as you don't niche down	Yes; lists of recurring clients are valuable	Yes	Yes	wpcurve.com
Recurring products	They can be more profitable than one-off products because of the higher LTV	Potentially yes; there are some huge markets available in physical products	Yes; having your own physical product and IP can be a great asset that is hard to replicate	It depends, but it is possible.	Yes	dollarshaveclub.com
Memberships	Difficult to scale; generally founder involvement is high	Generally not	Yes and no; so much founder involvement makes it less of an asset and churn is generally high	Yes	Yes	tropicalmba.com/innercircle/

Criteria	Profit margin	Large market	Asset	Simple	Recurring	Best practice example
Physical goods	Possible but not easy; margins are an issue, shipping is a challenge	Yes	Yes, assuming you are creating your own product.	It depends, but it is possible	No	backtotheroots.com
Info products	Good margins but often too reliant on the founder	Sometimes	Possibly, although they tend to have a short shelf life	Yes	They tend not to work too well as a recurring product	entrepreneuronfire.com/podcastersparadise
Local agency	No	No	Yes, if it's a good client list and you have a high % of recurring.	No	Some yes, some no. Not 100% recurring.	bluewiremedia.com.au
Consulting (project based)	Probably good but not scalable	Generally local in nature	No	Can be productized but generally isn't	Sometimes	The main ones are large corporate consultancies which aren't really relevant here

Criteria	Profit margin	Large market	Asset	Simple	Recurring	Best practice example
Freelancing (hourly)	Probably not great once you take into account the non-billable work	Possibly, although often price sensitive	No	Can be, but freelancers are often expected to do a wide range of things	Generally not	Most successful freelancers go on to start product-based businesses
Local restaurant	No	No	No	No	No	There are some obvious examples that have been able to scale, but most haven't
Franchisee	No	No	No	No	No	Franchises generally make good jobs but have little growth potential

For those of you on eReaders, the more green, the better. Otherwise, keep track of the yeses. If you can choose a business model that is all yeses and greens, then that's great. If not, you might have to go with some red and yellow while you build up the green percentage. Basecamp.com[55] started as a project web agency before they had enough revenue to drop the one-off work.

A local restaurant might pay you a nice founder's wage, but it's difficult to grow. Information products might give you big bursts of revenue, but a few years down the track your business may not have progressed.

Build growth elements into the DNA of your business and optimize for ongoing profit growth and asset value. In a few years you will have something valuable instead of a job that just pays reasonably well.

55 "Basecamp is everyone's favorite project management app," *Basecamp*, accessed July 21, 2014, https://basecamp.com/.

14 BUSINESS RULES TO LIVE BY

"The only way to win is to learn faster than anyone else."
Eric Ries

Hopefully I've set you on a path to create an exciting and profitable startup. The first major hurdle is launching; then, getting your first customer; and then, proving the concept and generating a wage for yourself in a scalable way. What happens after all that?

Now it's time to run your business, and your decisions from here out will make or break it in the long term.

Most businesses don't survive, so what do you do to keep yours growing?

Despite a lot of failures, I've managed to stay in business for eight years. Here are some of the personal philosophies that helped me get there.

1. Test Every Assumption

You are better off launching quickly and paying attention to real data rather than making assumptions. This doesn't just apply to launching; it's a general business principle that you can apply to almost every decision.

Most of the assumptions you have prior to and after launching your business will be wrong.

- Before the iPhone, people assumed you needed a keyboard or a stylus on your phone. Five years on, the BlackBerry and styluses are all but extinct.
- In the '70s people assumed no one wanted a computer in their home. Now everyone has a computer in their pocket and some people wear them on their wrist or their face!
- In the early 2000's people were happy copying their data to USB sticks. Now they use Dropbox.
- In the 2000's, people assumed mass market electric sports cars were impossible. 10 years later Tesla brought out the mass produced electric Model S and won car of the year.

Your assumptions don't have to be as dramatic. The business world is changing rapidly, small things don't get tested.

If you have an open mind, you can easily test your assumptions and those assumptions made by others in your industry.

- Why does everyone in your industry do things a certain way?
- What do your customers really like about your service?
- Why aren't people buying your product?
- Why *are* they buying your product?
- Are people using your product?
- How are they using it?
- Why do they love it?
- What do they tell people when they refer you?
- Are certain parts of your product necessary?
- Do you need an office?
- Do you need a business card?
- Do you need a logo?

Similar to the examples above, there may be assumptions in your industry that have prevented people from doing certain things. There's a very good chance they haven't been tested recently. One small discovery might be enough to kickstart a whole new business or product.

2. Solve Problems as They Arise

A lot of business owners spend time solving problems they don't have. Rob Walling refers to this as premature optimization. Examples include:

1. Getting a flawless credit card payment process setup before they have customers.
2. Optimizing their website before they have traffic.
3. Hiring staff before they have work for them.
4. Investing in the best systems before they have enough work to warrant it.

Normally these decisions stem from believing that when you have a problem, you won't be able to resolve it quickly. Yet this assumption is often wrong. Many of these issues can be resolved quickly. Here are some examples from our own business:

1. WP Curve had 200 recurring customers for our WordPress support business before it had a help desk. We were using Google docs, Trello, and a shared email inbox. When the business outgrew that system, it moved to a help desk system in one day.

2. I launched with an MVP site that I built myself for $77. Once I had proven the business and had enough traffic to the site (20,000 visits per month), my team invested $1,000 in a professional design and it was live within a week.

These days you can solve most business problems quickly. There's no reason to spend any time on problems you don't have. Doing so will only cost you valuable time and money. It will take attention away from the work you *should* be doing.

There's a good chance that if you are a new business, you only have one problem: not enough customers. That's where you should be spending your time.

3. Do What You Say You Will Do

Being true to your word is a very important part of building trust in business. Whether you are offering services or selling a product, make sure you always deliver on what you promise.

You can do everything else right, but if you are the guy or girl that promises the world and doesn't deliver, your mistake will be uncovered in the end. Your reputation is everything and it will impact every business you start, not just this one.

It's far better to under-promise and over-deliver, or at the very least deliver exactly what you promise every time.

4. Benchmark Against the Best

Launching quickly is important early on when the conditions are uncertain. Once you have a clear path, however, quality is more important. For example, with WP Curve, the first website took me three hours to put together. When it was clear the team was going ahead with the business, I put up a new site, and made sure it was well designed and faster than anyone else in the industry.

Any time you feel yourself wondering if what you are doing is good enough, compare it to the best:

- Don't ask your friends to pick between three logos. Instead, compare them all to Apple. If it's nowhere near as good, try again.
- If you write a blog post, compare it to one on KISSmetrics.com[56]. If it's not as good, rewrite it.

56 "The @KISSmetrics Marketing Blog," *KISSmetrics*, accessed July 21, 2014, http://blog.kissmetrics.com/.

- If you launch a website, compare it to bench.co[57] or simple.com[58]. If it's nowhere near as good, then you can do better.

It's often asking a lot for a small business to reach the levels of an established leader. You will be compared to leaders, and if you don't measure up, then people will notice.

By comparing yourself to the best, you set higher expectations for yourself, and you will be better for it.

57 "Bookkeeping services for your business," *Bench*, accessed July 21, 2014, https://bench.co/home/.

58 "Online Banking With Automatic Budgeting & Savings," *Simple*, accessed July 21, 2014, https://www.simple.com/.

5. Learn From Others and Yourself

Don't debate every last issue internally until you are blue in the face. Whatever you are discussing can probably be solved by either looking at what other companies have done before you, or implementing a quick decision and learning from the real data.

The minutiae that you are debating could be distracting you from a fundamental problem that you aren't seeing.

ALWAYS TAKE A STEP BACK AND ASK YOURSELF IF IT'S FEASIBLE THAT SOMEONE ELSE MAY HAVE SOLVED THIS PROBLEM BEFORE.

6. Outlearn Your Competition

Eric Ries says this best:

> *"Startups exist not just to make stuff, make money, or even serve customers. They exist to learn how to build a sustainable business. This learning can be validated scientifically by running frequent experiments that allow entrepreneurs to test each element of their vision."*

The companies that learn the quickest, win. This is partly because they do no not make decisions based on assumptions and partly because they learn from their predecessors. While your competitors are debating which assumption is better than the other, you can build a competitive advantage by gathering real information from your customers.

ERIC RIES CALLS IT "BUILD, MEASURE, LEARN." MICHAEL MASTERSON CALLS IT "READY FIRE AIM." I CALL IT "GETTING SHIT DONE."

7. Always Consider How Your Business Looks Without You

Don't believe that people should only work *on* their business and not *in* their business. It's crucially important that you do both.

However, you always need to be conscious of how your business will operate and grow without you. You'll naturally gravitate to things that you do well, but if your skills are hard to replace, you have to be careful.

An easy way to do that is to consider what happens when the business is, say, five times as big. WP Curve has rough estimates for:

- How many developers it will need (using an estimate of clients per developer).
- How many project managers it will need (using an estimate of clients per project manager).
- What payment fees, admin fees, and affiliate fees are per client.
- How much paid content creators will cost.
- How much a reasonable marketing expense is.

- How much a reasonable expense is for other items like conferences, video equipment, etc.

When putting all of this together, I can get some idea of the "real" margin in the business as it grows.

8. Look for Sources of Momentum

Do more of what is working. I've worked on over ten different business ideas and only one of them has really taken off. The best thing I've done is make sure my attention was focused on the one that had the momentum.

It would be easy for us to gloat in achieving what WP Curve has in the first year of business and think it's a result of the team's great work. The truth is: I have made big mistakes, just as regularly as I have with other failed businesses.

- I completely butchered our ideal client profile, spending months chasing the wrong kind of customer (most of them would later churn).
- The team spent four months selling to agencies for a grand total of a single $49 job, refuting one of the major assumptions I'd made launching the business in the first place.
- I had changed the pricing model regularly, only to change it back days later.
- I launched a bunch of new services, all of which failed and took away valuable time and attention from the core business.

Once momentum kicked in, these had little impact. In a job, this kind of incompetence would be grounds for dismissal and would cripple a lot of companies.

In fact, this past March WP Curve started the month by churning 22 of our paying customers for one failed product. This put the company at negative 6% growth on day one. Getting to 0% was going to be a struggle, not to mention hitting the 10% growth goal. However, by the end of March WP Curve had grown by 15%. Momentum got us there. People kept signing up.

Being part of a business that fails is tough. You feel like you are doing great work and you probably are. But no matter what you do, you can't win. You improve your product, up-skill yourself, talk to your customers, read books, change pricing… you name it. Success eludes you.

On the other hand, when things are on a roll, no matter how many mistakes you make, things keep going in the right direction. You screw up a few jobs, miss a few deals, waste time on the wrong things, get distracted. Things still power on.

I've been in both positions in the last 12 months. From losing 90% of my savings on a startup plagued with chronic failure to a business that was profitable in 23 days and signed up over 400 monthly clients in the first year or so. Doing more or less the same things.

Momentum is a powerful force, so keep an eye out for what is working and do more of it.

9. Manage Motivation

Your own personal happiness and motivation are the most important keys to the success of your business. I know plenty of people who have created great businesses, taken them to a point, and then lost all motivation.

If you are struggling with motivation, join a forum, start a mastermind, find a co-founder, hire people to do the hard work, and get back to what you're good at.

Take the warning signs seriously.

YOU SHOULD BE MORE EXCITED ABOUT MONDAY THAN YOU ARE ABOUT FRIDAY. IF THAT'S NOT THE CASE, THERE'S A GOOD CHANCE THINGS AREN'T GOING TO WORK OUT.

10. Cull Difficult Customers

Difficult customers will waste your time, kill your confidence, and destroy your motivation (and soul). No amount of money is worth working with a difficult customer.

Every difficult customer can be replaced by a better one, generally much quicker than you think. The work required to replace them is a far better use of your time than any work spent trying to help them.

My team prides themselves in sniffing out potentially difficult customers prior to sign-up and scaring them off. I also cheer when the team lets a bad customer go or they leave on their own accord. I want to work with good people, and my team values time and group sanity.

Normally it's simply people being unreasonable. Customers with high expectations are great because they can push your business forward, but some people are unreasonable and you a better off without them.

11. Focus on Retention

The only thing that will kill a recurring business is that more customers leave than sign up. It's hard to get new customers, but it's easy for them to leave.

You need to do everything to keep your customers and the data you get from churning customers is priceless.

Make sure you are delivering constant value for your existing customers. If someone does leave, don't send them a long and detailed survey, send them this—it's a Jay Abraham trick.

> *Subject: Did we do something wrong?*
> *Body: Hey [first name]*
> *I noticed you cancelled your subscription, did we do something wrong?*

Most people will reply to this and you'll find out the real reason people are leaving.

Figure out why and deal with any issues that arise.

12. Avoid Short-Term Thinking

Building a startup takes time. Chasing short-term projects or launches is easy, but it doesn't build an asset. Launching a whole bunch of related services will boost short-term revenue, but it will add complexity to your business that will hurt you in the long term.

Patience isn't something that many entrepreneurs have, so you might have to work on this one.

I've found two things that help:

1. Use a simple spreadsheet that predicts growth 12 months in advance. Seeing those numbers can be motivating and act as a good reminder that it will be worth waiting around.
2. Have an "abundance go to" saying. The one I used to tell myself early on was: "*There are 70,000,000 WordPress websites. Surely there are 500 of them who will pay $69/month to make sure they don't have to worry about their site.*" When you put it like that, it seems crazy to do anything other than continue focusing on building your business. This help with

motivation, but it also is a reminder that you don't need to chase other shiny objects.

Think in the long term about what asset you are building as a result of actions you complete today. Getting carried away on short-term projects will kill any chance of momentum and hurt growth.

13. Focus on Product

Running a business can be daunting. Every expert has a different opinion on some "must have" technique or technology you need to be using. It's hard to know where to spend your time, money, and attention.

If you are in doubt, come back to the product. Anything you can do that improves the product or improves the customer experience will be a sound investment.

If you are feeling overwhelmed with all of the things you need to do, just focus on how to make your product slightly better.

This is the best way to spend your time.

14. Love Your Work

If you don't, the rest will fall apart.

It's that simple.

EPILOGUE

WHERE TO GO FROM HERE?

I hope you've found this book a valuable tool for thinking about your startup. If you've had one idea while reading this book, or you've launched quicker than you would have, then I think it's been a success.

I hope you can avoid making the same mistakes I've made and launch an exciting and profitable startup the *first* time around.

I'm not talking about a business that has you "working for yourself." I'm talking about a business that serves as a vehicle for creation of something real and valuable.

Treat business advice with suspicion and test every assumption including your own. It's far more important to learn from your customers.

Understand growth and understand how your business looks without you, but don't be afraid to get your hands dirty.

Make difficult decisions early that lead to more growth and higher value later on. Look out for sources of momentum and keep doing what's working.

Listen to your customers and watch what they do.

Operate in a large market with a unique point of difference that responds to your customers' pain or pleasure points. It's a big world, and if you are smart about the way you structure your offering, there is unlimited room for growth.

Make a great product, do one thing well, and learn to say "no." It's your business. Constantly improve your product above all else.

Move quicker and learn faster than your competition.

Create something new, create something valuable, and have fun.

More Resources

I've included a bunch of resources to help you out with your startup journey. Please visit wpcurve.com/7daystartup to download them all for free.

You can also leave a comment up there and I'll continue to improve those resources over time.

Do You Mind Helping?

I have put this book out there for free and ask for nothing in return. However, if you do feel like helping out, you can do so by sharing wpcurve.com/7daystartup with friends or on social media, or leave me an Amazon review at wpcurve.com/amazon.

I'd really appreciate if you were able to do that, but only do it if you feel the book has helped you out.

Best of luck with your startup journey. I'd love for you to stay in touch with me. The best ways to do so are:

- Jump on my weekly email list at wpcurve.com/subscribe. I read and reply to all of my emails.
- Friend or follow me on Facebook at wpcurve.com/facebook
- Follow me on Twitter at @thedannorris or go to wpcurve.com/twitter
- Give us a shout on twitter.com/hashtag/7daystartup

ACKNOWLEDGEMENTS

To my wife, Caty. I told you we'd be rich by the time I was 30, but I sent you on an emotional rollercoaster and lost all of our money. Thanks for sticking with me. I'm sorry and I love you.

To my fo-founder Alex. I don't mention Alex much in this book because it's predominantly about what happened before we launched WP Curve. Alex has been my work wife for 12 months, together we've created something amazing, and become great friends. Thanks for jumping on board and keeping this ship stable.

Elisa Doucette and her team at writingbusinesswell.com edited my raw ramblings into something worth reading. Thanks for being patient and being a good friend.

Derek Murphy designed our cover and formatted the book. Thanks a million, I'm stoked with the outcome. Check out Derek's work at creativindiecovers.com.

I call Rob Walling The Oracle. He is the spiritual leader of the bootstrappers movement. Rob came in at the last minute to help with the foreword and I can't thank him enough.

Thanks to Brittany McClafferty and Janine Nesbit for supporting Alex and I and leading the WP Curve cheer leading squad.

Thanks to all of the entrepreneurs and groups who have inspired me over the years. I'd like to specially thank John Dumas, Chris Ducker, Brent Shepherd, The Dynamite Circle, James Schramko, Dan Andrews, Eric Ries, Steve Blank, Jason Fried and DHH from basecamp.com, Damian Thompson, Noah Kagan, Hiten Shah, Jason Calacanis, Matt Bellemare, Brendon Sinclair, Adam Franklin & Toby Jenkins.

Finally I'd like to thank the team of people who helped us review the book and who have commented or shared the content I've put out leading up to the book's release.

41361943R00118

Made in the USA
Lexington, KY
11 May 2015